Better Dads,
Stronger Sons

Better Dads, Stronger Sons

How Fathers Can Guide
Boys to Become Men
of Character

Rick I. Johnson

Revell
Grand Rapids, Michigan

© 2006 by Rick I. Johnson

Published by Revell
a division of Baker Publishing Group
P.O. Box 6287, Grand Rapids, MI 49516-6287
www.revellbooks.com

Repackaged edition published 2017
ISBN 978-0-8007-2870-0

Printed in the United States of America

The Library of Congress has cataloged the original edition as follows:
Johnson, Rick, 1956–
    Better dads, stronger sons : how fathers can guide boys to become men of character / Rick I. Johnson.
       p. cm.
    Includes bibliographical references.
    ISBN 10: 0-8007-3098-4 (pbk.)
    ISBN 978-0-8007-3098-7 (pbk.)
    1. Fathers—Religious life. 2. Fatherhood—Religious aspects—Christianity. 3. Fathers and sons—Religious aspects—Christianity. I. Title.
    BV4529.17.J64 2006
    248.8′421—dc22
                                         2005032016

18   19   20   21   22   23   7   6   5   4   3   2

To Frank and Kelsey.

Without you, none of this would have happened. I love you guys, and I'm proud to be your dad.

Contents

Acknowledgments

I'D LIKE TO thank Brian Smith, the best writer I know personally, for all his help with this book. I've also been blessed to have one of the most patient and gracious editors a writer could have, Dr. Vicki Crumpton. Thanks, Vicki, for your encouragement and unending patience with me as I stumbled along the rocky and very narrow path of authorship.

I'd also like to thank Steve Ziegler, Monte Edwards, and Tim Hart for their contributions to this book and for being good men.

Of course, Terry, Linda, Bill, and Brian, you all deserve a big "thanks." Without such a top-notch writer's group, how would I have ever ended up here? And thanks to George and Riley for being my constant companions during the days and nights of writing.

As always, Suzanne, you deserve most of the credit for any and all of my accomplishments.

Introduction

The Redemption of a Man

GOD DOES WORK in mysterious ways.

I was raised in an alcoholic home. I can distinctly remember lying in bed at night as a little boy, my little brothers and sisters huddled around me in fear, my pillow tightly pulled over my ears, desperately crying to God to make the fighting, screaming, and hitting in the next room stop. I prayed fervently, with all my heart and soul. But God didn't answer those prayers—then.

I grew up to be an abuser of drugs, alcohol, and any other substance that would deaden the pain I felt in my soul but didn't acknowledge. I slept with a multitude of women, never realizing that what I was really looking for was love, not sex.

I met my wife and married her when I was twenty-five. She unwittingly followed my masculine leadership into depths of degradation and despair. Finally, with the birth of my son when I was thirty, I recognized my foolishness and stopped taking drugs—the first step on the road to recovery. Years of counseling followed as I attempted to lead a "normal" life and be a good husband and father despite my lack of a positive role model growing up. By then I had substituted work and achievement (society's legal narcotics) for the numbing effect of drugs.

At forty, I had what the world said should have made me happy and satisfied. I owned a relatively successful business. I was married to a beautiful wife with two great kids, owned a nice house and new cars, and had money to burn. We weren't rich, but compared to most people we were living a pretty good life. I was what the world considers a success.

Yet I was miserable. The more I accomplished, the less gratifying my success was. I stubbornly adopted a "me against the world" attitude; I was going to win no matter the cost. I believed that *I* controlled my destiny and that all I needed to do was work harder and smarter to achieve my dreams and goals.

But I was trying to ignore a reality that undermined all my efforts. I had hypocritically compromised so many of my self-imposed principles that I had a hard time looking myself in the eye when I shaved in the morning. I despised who I had become. Not that I was a bad guy. In fact, by the world's standards I was considered a fairly good man. But I had a void in my soul that couldn't be filled, no matter how much I poured into it.

How could I have everything the world offers and still be so dissatisfied?

I remember thinking many times as I drove down the freeway how easy it would be to just turn the steering wheel a little to the right, hurtling my car into a telephone pole. Perhaps that would give me the relief I sought so desperately, putting an end to my feelings of despair and hopelessness.

That I didn't kill myself is a tribute to God's grace in my life, even while I still despised him. I told myself I resisted suicide because I didn't want to cause my wife and children to suffer, but the truth is, I was too cowardly to take my own life.

I finally decided to take inventory of my life and see if I could fix whatever was wrong with me. After all, that's how I had taken care of every other dilemma I had faced before. Since I had no men in my life whom I respected at the time, I decided to look at the lives of admirable men throughout history to determine what they had that I didn't.

As I researched the lives of brilliant men such as Leonardo da Vinci, George Washington, John Adams (and nearly all the other founding fathers of our country), Abraham Lincoln, and many others throughout the ages, the one common thread I discovered among them was that they were all Christians. I was shocked. I had grown up in a family that considered religion in general to be a crutch for weak people and Christians in particular to be a bunch of hypocrites.

In reaction to that revelation, I set out to prove to myself that Christianity was a false concept. I believed that the Bible was written by uneducated, superstitious savages and that the basis for believing in a mythical Jesus was one of unenlightened ignorance. I was a scoffer of the highest magnitude. In fact, I despised people who could so easily be led around like docile cows with rings in their noses.

After a year of research and study, I finally had to admit that I could not disprove Christianity. As illogical as I believed the concept to be, something about it spoke to me deep in my gut. In time I became convinced that Jesus Christ not only existed but was actually the Son of God who had come to earth as a man to die for our sins and rise again in order to provide eternal life for all who chose to believe and accept his gift.

So I believed. I took the gift. The decision was not based on emotion or one that someone talked me into but one based on logic and my own research.

Talk about a paradigm shift! My whole worldview was shaken and turned upside down. I thought, *So now that God has hunted me down and saved me, where do I go from here?* Someone told me I needed to start praying. I didn't know how to pray, and frankly, it was a little scary. I had prayed before, as a kid, and God had ignored me. But I decided that if I really believed in this God, I would be a hypocrite not to try to live by his guidelines. And in my family of origin, being a hypocrite was worse than being a Christian. So I began to pray.

In faith—for I really had no *reason* to believe prayer worked—I prayed every day for two things. First, that God would allow me to like myself, because I was convinced there was no way I could ever love myself. But if I could just like myself, I thought, things would be okay. At least I wouldn't want to kill myself anymore. And second, I prayed that God would bring some friends into my life. I was so lonely. I had many acquaintances but no real friends. Now, years later, God has blessed me so abundantly in both of those areas, far beyond my dreams and expectations. But that's a story I'll tell later in this book.

I soon realized that God had blessed me with a number of personal gifts or traits that I had been using only for self-gratification and that I needed to start using to serve him. I spent the next year trying different types of service—everything from ushering at church to picketing abortion clinics—hoping to figure out how God wanted me to serve him.

I was particularly concerned about the culture around me. How could our culture be so far off base from all the truths that I had recently learned to be self-evident? Our country seemed to be decaying at an accelerated pace. But I didn't know how one man could possibly make a difference in this troubled world. The task seemed overwhelming. At the same time, I was also deeply concerned about the kind of father I was. I kept searching for answers: how can a man become a good father when he has been raised without one or with a very poor role model? No one seemed to have the answers to the questions that plagued my soul.

In August 2000, my son and I attended a Promise Keepers event. Strolling through the resource tables in the mezzanine, I spied a small booth in the corner manned by the National Center for Fathering. Drawn like a moth to a flame, I discovered that they were offering a one-day course to train small group facilitators to teach men how to become better fathers. It hit me like a slap in the face: One man *could* make a difference! Helping men become better fathers would change their lives and the lives of their families. This was how I could change the world!

I quickly signed up to take the course. A few days later I received a telephone call from the NCF saying that unfortunately, only five out of the fifteen thousand men in attendance had signed up for the course. They could not afford to send someone out to Oregon to train so few. However, they did invite me to Kansas City to participate in an intensive three-day training program to learn not only how to lead the small groups but also how to give four-hour workshop training presentations to large groups of men. God spoke to me then and there, verifying that this was the way to use all the gifts with which he had blessed me.

The intent of NCF is that participants who receive this training start their own organizations in their home areas. So I started a ministry called Better Dads with a mission to inspire and equip men to be more involved in the lives of their children. I began giving presentations such as "Seven

Secrets of Effective Fathers" and "Authentic Men, Authentic Fathers" to church men's groups and in schools. Shortly thereafter, a counselor with one of the school districts approached me and said, "We have a lot of single mothers raising sons in our district, and they have questions about boys. Could you put a program together for them?" At first I refused. Working with women hadn't been part of my vision. However, after the counselor pointed out that "it is easier to raise a boy than to fix a man," I reluctantly agreed to put together a presentation titled "Courageous Moms: Raising Boys to Become Good Men." That program immediately became popular, and I began giving presentations to groups of women across the Northwest.

God works in our lives in ways we don't always understand. Several years previous to starting the single moms program, I had been working toward a degree from a local university. I needed one credit in writing to finish my degree. Not wanting to take the time to attend ten weeks of class, I decided to take an online writing class. Since I wrote technical reports for a living, I decided to add some variety by taking a fiction writing course. Surprisingly, the instructor of the course encouraged me to continue writing. Later, during a writer's conference, an editor asked about my occupation. I explained about Better Dads and how it had evolved into working with single moms raising boys. She became excited and requested a book proposal on the subject. That book and a request for this one soon followed.

And so that is how, at the age of forty-eight, I find myself attempting to pass on what God has shown me in hopes that other men will benefit and find hope from my experiences and failures. I am not a perfect father, as my kids would readily attest were I to give them access to these pages. In fact, I'm not even sure I'm a particularly good father. Compared to some men I know, I'm still ashamed at my lack of fathering skills. But perhaps that's the point. We will never be perfect fathers, none of us. But we mustn't let that stop us from becoming lifelong learners, continually striving to be the fathers God designed us to be.

Come with me while I share some of the things I've learned along the bumpy road to authentic manhood and godly fathering. A father's job never ends, and your son is counting on you.

1

Authentic Manhood

*A man is created for challenges. He is equipped to
overcome, to run the gauntlet, to stand firm as a
well-anchored corner post. Men are the benchmark
in life, society, and family. It is part of the masculine
responsibility to demonstrate strength and stability, to
protect and provide for those within their sphere of
influence. This is the hallmark of manhood.*

Preston Gillham, *Things Only Men Know*

ASK MEN ON the street, "What is a man?" and you'll get
a flurry of answers, few very definitive and few the
same. That's because most of us were never raised with a
clear vision of what a man is or exactly what a man does.
We were never shown our destiny.

As I look back on my life, especially the past five years,
I can clearly see God's work in my life to fulfill the plan he

established for me before time began. My journey toward becoming the man and the father God wanted me to be was long and arduous. One thing I've learned is that before we can become godly *fathers*, we must seek to become godly *men*. So before we discuss God's plan for you as a father, we might find it helpful to first determine exactly what a man is.

What Is a Man?

The world would have us believe that a man is one who finishes school, then puts his head down with his nose to the grindstone and works hard the rest of his life in order to achieve some level of monetary success. Along the way we acquire a wife and children, a home, fancy cars, clothes, and a plethora of toys in order to demonstrate our manly success to the world. Our work soon defines who we are and becomes a badge of honor in the world's eyes.

The problem with this mentality is that it believes an empty promise. After driving ourselves hard our whole lives, we suddenly wake up one day and realize that we have missed out on much of what is really important in life. Our kids are grown and gone, and we have drifted apart from the wife of our youth, or maybe even divorced her. Most men who follow the conventional definition of manhood typically die within a relatively short time span after retirement. Is that really how God wants us to live our lives?

Hardly. God has a better plan for our lives. Authentic manhood, or walking the path of godly intent, is living for a cause bigger than yourself. It means a life spent in servant leadership of others. A life spent lifting up your wife and children with the goal of helping them achieve their full potential. A life spent reaching out to others who need the support and shade of your broad shoulders. Men who live lives of significance are healthier and happier, and they look forward to a greater reward from our heavenly Father than their work-obsessed counterparts do. These true men shake off their natural tendency toward passivity, they accept responsibility, and they lead their families and communities courageously.

One of a man's greatest needs in life, especially as he approaches middle age, is to be involved in something significant—to know that his life has counted for something. This type of lifestyle requires us to shed some of the self-serving instincts that all men possess. Start living your life serving others and see if you don't become more content and have a strong feeling of significance. That is how God created men to live. That is what makes for a fulfilling life.

These are the makings of authenticity, of the life God wants us to live. It's a life that surpasses the mere satisfaction of our own needs and wants. A life that accomplishes even more than lifting up our wives and children to their full potential. A life spent impacting broader circles of people, reaching out with grace, compassion, and love to better the world we live in. That is Christ's assignment for men. Our lives are determined not by what we do but by what we do for others.

God created men to be the leaders in our families, homes, communities—the whole earth. However, he also gave us the responsibility that goes along with that. One of Satan's primary strategies against men is to convince us that the family is not important—that our own self-gratification is first priority. But authentic men know the true nobility that lies behind fulfilling our destiny.

Noble Fathers and Noble Sons

In order to fulfill God's commission of becoming authentic men and fathers, not only must we become men of action, we must become men of honor in the eyes of our sons. Those eyes are watching us constantly. They observe, among other things, how we react to the many injustices in the world. Do we ignore them and live a lie, or do we live *life*? Will we do something—anything—to make a difference in the world?

God loves men and created us to be something special—noble leaders. He created us in his image, to be like him. But God is never passive or complacent. Unfortunately, many men are living lives of complacency. We are abdicating our roles as leaders in our homes, our communities, and our country in record numbers. This is creating a crisis that is threatening to dissolve the very fabric of society, destroying our country and possibly even the world. Men in our country are mired in apathy and passivity. The reason? Because as boys, we were not brought up to relish our God-given roles as protectors of and providers for our families.

Men were created to be passionate and fierce and noble. We have a spiritual longing for adventure, for a battle to fight that's bigger than ourselves, for significance in our lives. We can feel that longing in our souls. We may not admit that to our wives or to other men, but we should be honest enough to admit it to ourselves. For most of us, something is missing. We long to do things that make us and others around us uncomfortable, to tackle insurmountable odds, to change the world. Instead, we trudge along in misery with the mundane lifestyle that the world says is our destiny.

We long in our very souls for significance, for something greater than individual success, material goods, sexual conquests, and even power. That's why men in their forties and fifties, after achieving what the world would consider success, are often struck with a sense of incompleteness. Midlife crisis isn't about buying expensive sports cars or chasing younger women, although that's how many men express it. Midlife crisis happens when it finally hits us that we have not really accomplished anything significant with our lives, that our names will never be remembered beyond a few words in an obituary, that we wasted the nobility that God gave us by chasing after material goods and transitory, self-gratifying experiences. Men who are living authentic lives receive God's blessings and don't feel the urge to relive their younger years. But these men willingly put themselves at risk by attempting to change the status quo. They fight injustice and help others instead of just serving their own carnal lusts. This is a mighty battle that requires men of nobility to go against their natural bent.

I used to feel overwhelmed at the magnitude of that battle. But to fight injustice in service of others, even if we fail, is not truly failure; it is faithfulness. And faithfulness always makes an impact, especially on the hearts of those who follow in our footsteps. A man who stands up to the winds of adversity is a man whose son admires and looks up to him. He is a man who will raise sons of whom he can be proud. Part of raising a noble son is to be a noble father.

God has shown me that one man can make a difference in the world, even if it's only in the life of one little boy. That one boy may grow up to impact thousands of people. That boy might even be your son.

In the movie *It's a Wonderful Life*, Jimmy Stewart plays George Bailey, a man trapped in the small town of Bedford Falls. He is dissatisfied with life because he is unable to fulfill his dreams. He is stuck because he is compelled to do the right thing by taking over his family's savings and loan business. George continually sacrifices his dreams for the benefit of others. Finally, during a crisis, he wishes he'd never been born, and his guardian angel reluctantly grants his wish. As George revisits the town and people he has known his whole life, he gradually realizes the impact he has made. With no one to lend money for middle-class family homes, the once pleasant town of Bedford Falls has been transformed into Pottersville, a modern-day Sodom and Gomorrah. Without George there to save his brother Harry from death during childhood, Harry never grew up to save the lives of hundreds of soldiers on a troop transport during World War II. George's wife is an old maid instead of the vibrant, beautiful mother and wife she is under his leadership. George's friends, relatives, and customers are all worse off, some even insane or in prison, for never having had his influence in their lives. One man (or woman) can make a difference in the world.

My wife's grandmother, Esther (Nana) Emry, was a quiet, tiny, crippled, poverty-stricken old lady. When I married my wife, I knew Nana was a strong Christian, but because of her low station in life and my own egotism, I never really paid much mind to her. However, over the years I've come to see how this shy little old lady impacted the lives of thousands of people. In fact, she is still impacting people long after her death and will for generations to come.

Because I believed that all Christians were hypocrites, I watched Nana with a skeptic's eye. She was the first believer I had ever met who actually walked the talk of Christianity. She was truly filled with grace and humility.

Nana raised six children with no husband long before celebrities made single-mothering trendy. She took in my wife, who left home at age thirteen, and instilled a Christian value system in her. She also took in a hodgepodge of other stray kids over the years, allowing them a place to stay and gather their bearings. Most of these kids she fed cheese sandwiches with cheese sliced so thin you could see through it and soup stock made from boiled chicken bones. But what she had, she shared joyfully and without expectations.

Nana never had much money, existing on a small Social Security check. Yet I never once in twenty years heard her complain about anything. She faithfully tithed and gave sacrificially every month until the day she died, even though she was too crippled to attend church. She made quilts from scraps of material and sent them all over the world to various missions and needy people. She was a strong prayer warrior. She prayed every day, thanking God for the gift of one more day on earth, despite a body wracked with pain.

When my wife, as a young woman, would run to Nana crying about her jerk of a husband (me), Nana would only say, "Oh, just love him, honey. Just love him." She never criticized me or gave any other advice, much to Suzanne's frustration. Nana just did exactly what the Bible exhorts—that older women teach the younger women to love their husbands (see Titus 2:4).

Consequently, Nana was a deciding factor in my decision to accept Christ as my Savior. That decision has impacted my children and will impact their children too. It also affects every life I touch through my ministry and books. I sincerely pray that I can live up to the legacy Nana left in my life. I look forward to meeting her in heaven to thank her and to witness all those many others whose lives were somehow made different by this quiet, unassuming little old lady as they gather around her formerly crippled feet in gratitude. I suspect Nana was surprised and humbled that God threw a party in her honor when she passed on to heaven.

God truly does work through people we wouldn't expect. He will work through you too if you'll stand up and say, "Lord, use me."

Questions for Reflection and Discussion

1. Are you living a life of significance? If you have any doubts, ask your son his opinion (and prepare yourself to listen without taking offense).

2. Discuss areas of your life that you struggle with now or have struggled with in the past. Be honest! Do you think these involve attacks from the evil one or just naturally occurring events in life?

3. In what ways are you resisting passivity in your life? In what areas do you feel you could improve? Talk to the other men in your group about ways you can each make a difference in someone else's life.

4. Try to envision what your community and the lives of people you know would be like if you were not present in their midst. Would your community be better off without you, or would it be more like "Pottersville" without your current activities?

2

Authentic Fatherhood

It is much easier to become a father than to be one.
Kent Nerburn, *Letters to My Son*

MEN, YOU ARE the leaders of your families. You might be reluctant to assume that role. You might even deny that it falls to you. Nonetheless, you *are* your family's de facto leader, whether you choose to believe it or not.

Leaders are always the highest-priority targets in any war. The enemy knows that if he can kill the commander, the troops will be easier to defeat. Cut off the head and the body dies. The body in this case is your family—you are the head. One way to fight back and be the leaders God created us to be is to be aware of our roles, our responsibilities, and our influence with those we lead.

The Indispensable Father

You may not think of yourself as being particularly influential or even successful in life. Maybe you don't make a lot of money, lead a large group of people, save lives, or invent amazing gadgets. Maybe life has even beaten you down, and you've lost confidence in your abilities. Consequently, you don't think of yourself as a big deal. But you can bet your boy does. He thinks you're a very big deal. He doesn't know or care what the outside world thinks. He only knows that between the walls of your home, you are about the biggest, wisest, most powerful person alive. Oh, he knows you're not perfect. But he doesn't care, because you're just good enough to be indispensable in his life.

Fathering is at the heart of masculinity, of what it means to be a man. Godly fathers put others' needs before their own. If you're like me, you spend the majority of your conscious thought and effort on satisfying your own wants and needs. It's almost an automatic response to life. But if we are to be authentic men and fathers, we need to rethink that attitude and consciously make sacrifices so others can benefit and prosper.

When fathers neglect this duty or are absent from the home, families are attacked by predators. Young men, such as gang members, who are raised without the influence of older men often become marauding wolves themselves—predators preying on women and children for their own self-gratification.

Families are like flocks of sheep. Children, like lambs, are naive and simple in their understanding of the world. Fathers are like sheepdogs, guarding the flock from marauding wolves. We protect our families from human predators and from corrupt television programs, movies, music, books, friends, and other people or influences that enter into a child's life.

By the way, sheepdogs come from the wolf genus, so they are no stranger to wolves' traits and habits. Fitting, isn't it? We dads often find the hackles rising on our necks when we sense a wolf in sheep's clothing parading around our kids. I once told my teenage daughter, "I might not always know why, but I know a wolf when I see one; I can sense him." Of course, my daughter says that I think *all* boys are wolves, but I just tell her that's because I used to be one. It takes one to know one.

When I was dating, I was, like all young guys, deathly afraid of the fathers of the girls I went out with. If the majority of fathers showed any interest in meeting the boys their daughters were dating, I suspect that nearly all young men would be forced to remain celibate until marriage.

The other day I stopped by an apartment complex to visit a young boy whose single mother had asked me to meet with him. As I pulled into the large complex, I noticed at least thirty-five or forty kids playing in the parking lot. The kids were of all ages, from toddlers up to teenagers. Several of the older boys were wearing gang attire, aggressively posturing, smoking pot, and swearing loudly. A number of young ladies wearing suggestive clothing were hanging around them, trying to get their attention. Rap music was blaring from a speaker for all the kids to hear, no matter how young. The lyrics of the song were so vulgar that they would have embarrassed the sailors on the Navy ship I was once stationed on. Yet these children played amidst this chaos as if it were a normal part of growing up. The only adults around were a few predatory men who skirted the perimeter of the action, looking for weakened prey.

My first thought was, *What chance do these children have of growing up to lead normal, productive, happy, and fulfilled lives?* My second thought was, *Where are the adults? Where are all the men?* When I spoke to the mother, I learned that no men were around because *no men live there* except the few I noted earlier scanning the flock for victims. I had just entered the realm of fatherless America.

I came by the apartment complex several weeks later, on a weekend. Many children were out playing, but this time four or five visiting fathers were out interacting with and supervising them. This time there were no predators lurking about, no gang attire, no drugs, no loud rap music, no half-naked girls, and no swearing. What a difference positive male influence makes. It was as if the sun had come out over the courtyard.

Fathering is a modeled behavior that is becoming an increasingly rare commodity today. Because of the high divorce rate in our culture, we have a generation of fathers who grew up without fathers of their own. Men have become fathers without ever having seen how a father acts and what his role entails.

Before I became a Christian, I was concerned about my fathering skills. Not having had a very good role model growing up, I was not exactly sure of what to do in certain situations. I found myself reacting instead of having a proactive game plan. Reacting to situations often forced me to use anger instead of wisdom. Even after I started reading books to improve my fathering skills, I was not confident in my abilities. The books encouraged looking for "teaching moments" to use for lessons. I wasn't sure what a teaching moment was, much less what to say or do when it came along. Thus I found myself evading or walking away from my responsibilities, thinking I was avoiding failure. I knew my children not only expected a better father but deserved one. And I knew my wife was watching and evaluating my role as a father. The prospect of losing her respect was more than I wished to endure. But by walking away from my responsibilities and trying to avoid failing actively, I was still failing. I was just failing passively, which was even worse!

Many men I talk to have the same feelings of inadequacy regarding their fathering abilities. Without the proper training and role modeling, fathering can seem like an overwhelming responsibility. But as author Frank Pittmon says, "The guys who fear becoming fathers don't understand that fathering is not something perfect men do, but something that perfects men. The end product of child raising is not the child, but the parent."[1]

Let me say this: you are the man God chose to be the father of your children! God could have picked anyone on earth for this task, but in his infinite wisdom, he chose you. Even if you don't have confidence in your fathering skills, God says you fit the bill perfectly for his plan for your family. He knows all your strengths and weaknesses, and he determined before time began that you would be the father of your children.

Does that make you feel better, or just more terrified? Relax—if you are reading this book, you are seeking knowledge and wisdom on how to become a better dad. That speaks well of your heart. If you are sincere and persevere, God will honor that worthy desire by working in your life to grant you that wish. I prayed many times to my heavenly Father for wisdom in raising my children, and I began to feel as though he had started honoring that request. Slowly but surely, I found myself recognizing "teaching moments" when they occurred. And by God's grace, he spoke through my mouth on many of those occasions—surprising even me with the wisdom that popped out! Once I began living a life of *intentional* fathering instead of just *reacting* to what life threw at me, God began blessing my efforts.

Today, I love being a father. For years I dreaded the thought of parenting teenagers. Now, however, I find the challenges of raising teenagers to be exhilarating—even though these years are typically the most unsatisfying for a father. The natural curiosity teens have about life. The hormonal highs and lows. Launching them into the world as productive, happy adults. Believe it or not, I find all of these to be *fun*, though challenging, and I find great satisfaction when God gives me the wisdom to address these needs.

He can give you the same fulfillment in your family. Keeping a good attitude is half the battle.

Believe me when I say I know how tough it is being a man and a father today. You feel like you give and work and struggle and there's never enough of you to go around. The pressures are unrelenting. And yet you are so important that you are nearly irreplaceable in the lives of your children—especially your son. Fatherhood is a privilege given by God, and with that privilege comes the power to impact lives. Exercised responsibly for good, that power can lead to God's blessing on you and your family.

Privilege, power, responsibility, sacrifice. They're all part of the same package. They all belong to a father.

Be a man. Stand tall. Give your son an example of masculinity that will survive down through the generations. I've heard men speak in reverent tones of their grandfathers or even great-grandfathers they've never met. The power of the masculine legacy they left behind has cured and hardened down through the ages like a concrete foundation of manliness.

The Power of Fathers

> The father receives his power from God (and from his own father).
>
> Alice Miller, *For Your Own Good*

Are fathers really all that important? Dr. James Dobson believes that our very survival as a people will depend on the presence or absence of masculine leadership in millions of homes across the country.[2]

But being a good father isn't about what kind of parent you are as much as it is about what kind of person you are. What kind of character do you have? How do you approach life and your responsibilities as a father?

Fathers have an innate ability to influence their children and the community around them. I call it "Father Power" in my workshops for men. It's not the physical power of being bigger and stronger than their wives and kids but the generational power with which God has endowed them—the power that allows fathers to affect people's lives positively or negatively, for good or evil, for hundreds of years. A father will impact people he doesn't even know and will never meet. Stu Weber says,

> The great river of fathering that leaped from the primordial mist of Eden rolls through time and into eternity. How will you bend the course of the tributary that flows in your family? You will *affect* it, you know. Whether you work at it with all your heart and soul or close your eyes and ears and put your hands in your pockets and pretend it doesn't exist, you will channel that river in one direction or another. That's the nature of fathering. You can't hide from its potency and power. Whether you like it or not, whether you accept it or not, whether you *believe* it or not, your influence will span generations long after you've left this earth.[3]

For instance, if a man sexually molests or abuses his son or daughter, the abuse will adversely affect that child's whole life. In all likelihood, it will also affect *that child's* children's lives as he or she exhibits the same abusive behavior. And so on it goes throughout the generations until someone courageously breaks the cycle of pain and finds healing. Conversely, men who father intentionally and put their children's needs ahead of their own start a legacy that snowballs with positive ramifications down through the centuries.

I know one woman whose lineage has been fraught with fatherlessness since her great-grandmother's time. As a result, each successive generation of young women have themselves become unwed teenage mothers. The legacy is passed on from generation to generation of daughters. These women's desperate search for masculine love and affection causes them to make choices that confuse sex with love.

So what is this power that fathers seem to possess yet are clueless about or unwilling to acknowledge? I know of no man or woman, regardless of age, who doesn't still yearn for his or her father's approval and love. I've met seventy-five- and eighty-year-old men and women whose only regret in life is that they never heard their father say, "I love you," or "I'm proud of you." That is a huge power.

Stu Weber states it this way: "There are two ways to recognize power. One is to see it at work. The other way is to measure what happens when it is gone. Either way, Dad is pretty potent. Present or absent. Positive or negative. The power of a father is incredible. . . . There isn't much of anything in life children can't face with Dad's strong hand wrapped tightly around theirs."[4]

Another power that God has endowed us with is the power to create life. No man should plant his seed in a woman, impregnating her, if he is not willing to accept lifelong responsibility for the child he created. With the power to create comes accountability. God holds you responsible and accountable for the welfare of your family. Maturity in a man begins not with age but with the acceptance of that responsibility.

As fathers we have the power to impact generations of lives. Make sure your impact on the twenty-first century is a positive one.

Spiritual Leaders

The great doers of history have always been men of faith.

Edwin Hubbel Chapin

I once heard of a man who went into his daughter's room and prayed over her every night after she fell asleep. She grew up and left for college. The following Christmas she came home for a visit.

Talking to her mother one afternoon, she said, "Daddy still prays for me every night even though I'm away at college, doesn't he?"

"How in the world did you know that?" her mother replied.

The daughter replied with confidence, "I can still see his knee marks in the carpet next to my old bed."

Were you blessed to have had a father who prayed faithfully for you when you were growing up? Only a small percentage of men I ask answer yes. How do you think your life might have been different if you had had a father who did that?

Try this experiment: go into your kids' room at night, kneel down, lay hands on their heads or backs, and petition God's blessings upon them. You'll find it a powerful moment. Your kids will stay very still under the blankets because, big or small, they recognize the significance of that act.

A pastor also once told me to pray not only for my own children's purity but for their future spouses' purity as well. And he said to pray for their future spouses' parents, that they would have wisdom to raise their children within God's laws. I've never forgotten that advice.

When your children know you are praying for them, for their sexual purity, and for the purity of their future spouse, this knowledge gives them a guidepost to hang on to. It also provides a form of accountability more powerful than bare parental authority.

The purpose of drawing close to God is not only to discern our destiny but also to lead our family and those closest to us to salvation. Part of our role as leaders of our families is to be spiritual mentors for our wives and children. It's the responsibility I felt least adequate to fulfill when I accepted Christ into my life. But God is more interested in what you can become than in what you are now. Interestingly, I found that my wife and children willingly followed my lead into spiritual growth—no matter how pathetic my efforts as a teacher and guide.

Shortly after becoming a Christian, I was blessed to join Good Shepherd Community Church in Gresham, Oregon. Stu Weber is the senior pastor of this church. Stu wrote such manly books as *Tender Warrior* and *Four Pillars of a Man's Heart*, and he was a big influence in my growth as a man and a father. I used to remark to my wife that listening to one of *Stu's* sermons was like eating a big, steaming-hot bowl of *stew* on a cold and rainy afternoon—it always left me full, contented, invigorated, and satisfied.

Our odyssey to Good Shepherd was probably not unusual. We had visited many churches over the previous ten years. Even though I wasn't a believer during that time, I thought it was good for my children to be exposed to Christian values. At several churches, we stayed for a year or so. In most of those cases, we suspect that no one knew we were attending, as they never approached us. Certainly no one seemed to notice when we left.

One weekend while my wife and I were away on a business trip, a young woman named Amy baby-sat our children, taking them to attend a Good Shepherd service. When we got back, the kids clamored for us to "check out this awesome church." After a month or so, we decided to visit Good Shepherd.

The pastor preaching that day, Randy Alcorn, gave a blistering sermon on the sanctity of human life, especially regarding the unborn. It was so convicting that my wife got up and walked out in the middle of the service. All in all, a rather inglorious start with our new church family.

As God would have it, the church was having a pastors' reception that evening for new members. I decided that any church willing to offend potential members in order to strongly promote an ideology they believed to be true was worth another look. (I think the Holy Spirit had a lot to do with my decision too.) At the risk of incurring my wife's wrath, I took her to the reception. At that reception, the authenticity of the three pastors in attendance was so strong that I was drawn toward it without reservation.

While my wife was not particularly happy at the time about my decision to attend the pastors' reception—or my subsequent decision for us to become church members—she readily followed my decisions in these spiritual matters.

Now, please understand that I was not a wise, mature Christian. I was a baby Christian in every sense of the word. The fact that she followed me speaks not only to her character but also to the importance women place on men becoming spiritual leaders in their homes. I've heard it said that the number one complaint of women in the church is their husbands' spiritual apathy. Pastor Jan Hettiga once said, "The number one problem in the church is the explosive combination of masculine apathy and feminine discontent." I submit to you that masculine apathy is the *cause* of feminine discontent. This apathy and lack of involvement is a problem for men not only in church but also in the home. It's an all-pervasive trend that we *must* break.

Fathers also play a significant role in passing on a spiritual foundation to their children—especially sons. When only mom takes her sons to church while they're growing up, approximately 15 percent of boys remain churchgoers after they become adults. However, if dad takes an active role with mom in leading the family to church, the number who continue their spiritual journey increases to somewhere around 75 percent.[5] That's a significant difference that speaks to the power men have to be spiritual influences upon their sons.

Many men are reluctant or even scared to lead their families spiritually. I harbored many doubts early on. *What do I know about theology? I'm not worthy of such a huge task that has eternal consequences. What if I mess up?* I was so scared that I was searching for ways to evade this responsibility.

In the summer of 1998, at the age of twelve, my son asked me to take him down on the field during a Promise Keepers event so he could accept the Lord. I tried making excuses why we shouldn't go, but Frank wouldn't accept my foot-dragging. When we finally approached one of the volunteers, he said to me, "Why don't you lead your son to the Lord?" Gulp! *What do I say?* After much stumbling around, I managed to murmur enough of a prayer to help Frank accept Christ into his heart. Since then, I've been blessed to watch his spiritual growth as a Christian, and someday I'll see him as a mighty man of God. I was subsequently blessed to baptize my wife and both our children—a truly humbling and awesome experience. God honored my feeble attempts at spiritual leadership by giving me these blessings.

Watch and see what blessing he has stored up for you. Grab the helm and lead your family spiritually!

God and Fathers

Finally, what does God say about fathers? God could have had any role he wanted, but he chose to be our heavenly *Father*. He could have called himself any name he wanted. In several passages in the New Testament, Jesus prays to God, calling him *Abba*, and urges others to do so as well. *Abba*, literally translated, means "Daddy"; it was the term of endearment used by a young child. Think of the implications behind that. Quite frankly, it scares me to think that I have been bestowed with a title that God claimed for himself.

We have several newborn babies in our church congregation. I love to watch the fathers hold their babies and interact with them face-to-face. It's a good allegory of our relationship with God. Here is a totally defenseless little human, completely at the mercy of a greater being, dependent upon him for survival. The baby simply sits and basks in the love being showered upon him by his daddy. The infant cannot yet understand the bigger picture of life, but he comprehends with full clarity the nonverbal message of love he receives from this powerful figure.

Besides the fact that God calls himself "Father," in what other ways are fathers connected with God? The Bible is God's way of truthfully speaking to us. According to my keyword search, the term "father" is used 1,488 times in the NIV Bible. Do you think God was trying to tell us that he considers fathering to be important?

Jesus had ultimate authority on earth, derived from God the Father. God has granted men power as leaders in the family. But with that power comes responsibility—the responsibility to learn about and use that influence for blessing our families. Unfortunately, many men today have abused that responsibility and thrown away that authority. Yes, I understand that some men do not deserve the mantle of family leadership. But society's attack on fathers is not the answer. As C. S. Lewis said, "to banish the knight does not alleviate the suffering of the peasant."[6]

I don't think it's coincidence that the last words God spoke to his people at the end of the Old Testament—his last words for four hundred years—were on the importance of fathering: "And he will turn the hearts of the fathers to the children, and the hearts of the children to their fathers, lest I come and strike the earth with a curse" (Mal. 4:6 NKJV).

God could have used any sign of societal revival to fulfill that prophecy. He could have said, "when people return to church," or "when there is no more hunger or war." But he chose to highlight the restoration of fathers to their children in connection with the return of the Lord.

The Hebrew word for *curse* in this verse is one of the harshest in Scripture, suggesting complete annihilation. That means only when men stop abdicating their God-mandated role as leaders in their families and communities will we be able to survive and thrive as a nation once again and not risk complete annihilation.

Here's the good news, though: God has a plan for you as a father and as a man. God chose you to lead your son, to make him a noble man. He didn't choose you and then leave you on your own to fail. Trust that God will help you if you seek his wisdom and discernment. Kindle the hope in your heart that God will work through you if you allow him to.

Then stand back and enjoy the results.

God's Blessings for the Journey

In those early days, I didn't know what I was doing half the time. But I blundered ahead anyway, praying the whole way and hoping God would turn my efforts into something eternal. And he did. He blessed me because I took action. I did not let my fear paralyze me. Just consider the ways that he has blessed me.

I went from being unhappy, stressed, uncomfortable around people and in many situations, confused, hopeless, scared, and miserable with life to having a wife who not only loves me but respects and admires me! She actually tells me she admires me. How cool is that? That has improved every aspect of our relationship—and I do mean *every* aspect.

When it comes to marriage, my only model growing up was a failure. I've now been married twenty-four years. That's not possible except through the grace of God.

I went from having almost no fathering skills (again, I was programmed to fail) to having kids who respect me and believe that I have at least a little wisdom—on even-numbered days of the month, anyhow.

God took me out of my virtual isolation and gave me rich, full friendships with dozens of men. I even have men regularly seeking my guidance. I'm amazed at the way people often go out of their way to help me. I believe these relationships are God's blessings for my commitment to living with authenticity.

My family and I now have hope instead of despair. My wife and kids are following in my footsteps, and I expect them to pass on a positive legacy for generations to come.

Remember how I said in my introduction to this book that God did not answer my prayers to stop the fighting and screaming and hitting—then? Well, he has answered those prayers now. None of that takes place in my home—though only through God's grace, because I had such a bad model set for me.

And one of the most gratifying blessings God has bestowed on me? Sometimes men and women come up to me after they've attended my seminars and share tearfully that God spoke through me and helped change their lives and the lives of their families for the better. I can't tell you what that feels like, except that it has to be a tiny glimpse of heaven. It fills my heart to bursting.

I enjoy all of these blessings because I overcame my initial fear and reluctance to try something that made me uncomfortable. I swallowed hard and chose to become a better husband and father and a godly man—a man who seeks God's strength to live a life of significance, helping others by sharing God's grace in a nonthreatening manner. God used my pitiful efforts for great good. He has since used my mustard seed of faith to accomplish more than I will probably ever know.

Be a bold, authentic dad, and step out in faith. God is anxious to use you and your son mightily.

Questions for Reflection and Discussion

1. In what ways has God endowed you with power, as a man and a father, to impact other people's lives?
2. In what ways are you fulfilling your role as a spiritual mentor to your wife and children? In what areas do you feel you could improve? If you have enough courage to hear the answer, discuss this question with your wife.
3. Think about what your father was like. Talk to your son about your relationship with your father when you were growing up. If you did not have a father, tell your son about the things you missed by not having a dad.
4. Talk to your son about the responsibilities of fathers. Talk about the rewards that come when a father fulfills his God-given role and the consequences when he doesn't.

3

Coming to Terms with the Past

> *As we try to change, we will discover within us a*
> *fierce struggle between our loyalty to that battle-*
> *scarred victim of his own childhood, our father, and*
> *the father we want to be. We must meet our child-*
> *hood father at close range: get to know him, learn to*
> *forgive him, and somehow, go beyond him.*
>
> Augustus Y. Napier, *The Fragile Bond*

No man can live a life of great impact or even a life of true fulfillment without coming to terms with and understanding his history. In order to be effective fathers, we must reconcile our relationship with the men and women who raised us, or we're doomed to repeat the same mistakes with our children.

You and Your Father

When I was twelve, during one of my parents' drunken late-night arguments, I found out that my stepfather was not my "real" father. Until then I had just naturally assumed that he was my biological father, and no one told me any different. It was a devastating blow to me at the time. Our relationship until then had seemed tense and a little strained, but not necessarily abnormal. However, from that point forward it seemed as if a dam had broken, and he mocked and criticized me until I grew to a size that made those actions imprudent. This criticism caused a loss of self-assurance in me, which subconsciously prompted me to try to overachieve to prove to him that I was worthy. It also made me feel inadequate in front of him.

For instance, the only conference wrestling match I lost in high school was during my sophomore year. Not coincidently, that match was the only one my stepfather ever attended. I lost 2–0 to an opponent I should have beaten handily. During the match I wanted to perform, but I just froze—my body literally wouldn't move! My coach was so mad at me, he nearly kicked me off the team. But how could I explain to him the paralyzing lack of self-confidence my stepfather's presence created in me?

Until you understand how your upbringing affects you today, you cannot father intentionally. Otherwise, all those problems get passed right down to your son. Author Ken Canfield says, "Fathers, damaged by their fathers, pass on the broken baton to their own sons."[1]

Whether you have a great relationship with your father or you despise him, it's vitally important for your own growth as a father to resolve any issues in your relationship, especially if your goal is to raise noble sons. In other words, you must reconcile with your father in order to become a better dad to your own son.

Try to remember the good things your father taught you and pass those on to your son. That kind of modeling is the way adult males have always taught boys to become men. It's not the telling as much as the showing. Just spending time together showing a boy what a man does and how he acts is what's most important. My stepfather and I never threw a baseball, hunted or fished together, worked on cars, or spent any significant time together doing anything. Despite his faults, my stepfather lived up to his responsibilities as a provider. In retrospect, I realize I never truly understood what it meant to be a man or how a man acts, except that he works and provides.

If you were fortunate enough to have had a good father while growing up, realize that you have truly been blessed by God. Make sure to tell your father how much you appreciate that gift before it's too late. I have several friends who grew up with good parents but take them for granted. That has always seemed a little selfish to me. Believe me, you have been blessed. Your open appreciation of that gift validates it in your son's eyes and makes your efforts that much more credible.

> ### Reconciling with Your Father
>
> 1. Pray for God to help you forgive and understand your father.
> 2. Approach your father with an open heart.
> 3. Find common ground—don't condemn him with the past.
> 4. Ask about his childhood and relationship with his father.
> 5. Tell him you want to have a deeper relationship with him.
> 6. Tell him that you love him—ask for his forgiveness if necessary.
> 7. Honor him as God would command.
> 8. If your father has died, write him a letter from your heart. Share it with your mother, if appropriate.

My friend Monte is a great hunting, hiking, and camping buddy, as well as a fellow warrior in God's army. Monte's one of the good ones. He wrote this touching story about his father and the bond they share that is passed from generation to generation.

My father was a patient fisherman. The fish would nibble, nibble, and he would wait. It would nibble some more, and still he waited. "Come on Dad, he's gonna get away."

"Be patient, son—he's just bumpin' it. Ya need to wait until he takes it in his mouth." And so, when his timing was right—when his "secret sense" would prompt—with a swift and fluid motion, he would set the hook as the curve of his pole forecasted the fight ahead. With a confident poise, he would battle the fish until it reluctantly surrendered to our net.

We would often fish in the evening after work. My father would call up and say, "I'll be home in an hour—get the gear ready." I'd always double-check to make sure we had the mosquito juice and the freshly cured salmon eggs out of the freezer. These small oversights had ruined trips before.

The midnight sun of Alaska created the long evenings that allowed us to pursue, with great success, the Red, the Silver, and the King Salmon. While everyone else would fish down at Soldotna Creek or at the bridge or the campground, we fished at a secret spot at the end of Poppy Lane. Our 1964 Ford pickup truck—the one with the spare tire mounted on the front bumper—would rumble down the dirt road to a rusty red gate. An ominous sign, which threatened bodily harm for trespassing, blocked our way—but my father had a key and permission to ignore the barrier. A half-mile past the gate and a few hundred yards down the trail was our favorite hole on the Kenai River. I always felt a special pride as we locked the gate behind us. "This is our secret spot—just me and my dad—serious guy stuff goin' on here."

I would watch my father to see how he handled his gear; how he tested the water and surveyed the conditions; and how he determined the correct setup that would land the biggest fish. Like battlefield generals, we would stand together on the bank overlooking the river to determine our "plan of attack." As I looked down his arm, like looking down the barrel of a rifle, he would point to a spot on the river. "Ya see where the white water makes a line next to that snag—I'll bet there's somethin' sittin' right in there." The weight of his hand on my shoulder confirmed his affection, and the smell of Old Spice and cigarette smoke still take me back to that place. A successful catch would flavor the trip home with a magical excitement as we anticipated a triumphant welcome and the adoration of our family.

I learned everything I needed to know about being a man on those fishing trips. While explicit instructions were never given nor weighty subjects discussed, the lessons were learned and the character was developed. Set your plan, weigh the options and make the best decision, and when the time is right, move with precision and confidence. The rewards of success are received with a humble confidence that speaks for itself. Always close the gate behind you—the burden of privilege is always repaid. Never leave a mess—a man always takes care of his own business. The joys of love and fellowship are the best rewards of all. I am my father's son. . . .

. . . On a frosty eastern Oregon morning on the opening day of deer hunting season, my son Bryan and I moved quietly along the ridge where I had shot a nice four-point the previous year.

"Dad, what about this spot? You can see down to the bottom of the ridge."

Squatting down, I pinched a small wad of dust and let it drop. "Ya see, the wind is at our backs—he's gonna wind us before we can get off a shot."

Continuing our search for the perfect morning stand, we surveyed several other spots on the ridge. Standing together we analyzed the terrain, tested the wind, and

45

discussed the pros and cons of each location. When my own "secret sense" prompted, we stopped and waited . . . and watched. In whispered tones, we discussed nothing and everything as the earth gave birth to a new day. This particular morning was only unsuccessful for deer—all other things were just as they should be.

Sometimes, out of the corner of my eye, I see my son looking at me. I know he's watching—as I watched. When I am tempted to make a profane judgment or leave a mess or show disrespect, I pause and know that my actions speak louder than my words. The "Wisdom of the Ages" is only communicated through deeds.

Last year, I followed as Bryan led the way. We had exercised his first preference for a prime hunt in the Malheur Unit, and only he carried a rifle. At the end of an old road, a marvelous clear cut stretched out before us. As we stood looking around, I spotted a small outcropping a quarter mile away. I raised my arm to direct his eyes, and Bryan leaned close to follow the angle of my point. "Ya see where the trees thin out above those rocks—the deer are gonna come right over the top to feed when the sun goes down." I paused for a moment at the realization that I had come full circle, and I felt the warmth of another time and another place. I thought I could smell the slight scent of Old Spice on the wind.

At the top of the clear cut, we looked back at the spot we had stood a half hour earlier. Without speaking, my son squatted down and grabbed a pinch of dust. As it fell he softly said, "Ya see, the wind is right in our face. This is gonna be a good spot." The joys of love and fellowship are the best rewards of all. I am my son's father.[2]

Honor Your Father and Mother

Offering forgiveness allows us an opportunity to honor our parents, even under the most difficult of circumstances.

The Bible tells us to honor our mothers and fathers. But what if you were raised by a mother or father who acted in ways that make it difficult to honor them? What are some practical ways you can follow God's commandment and receive the blessing attached to it?

One of the most important ways to reconcile with your father is to forgive him for any hurts, real or perceived, that you have from your childhood. Holding a grievance against another only harms us. It seldom hurts the other party. My experience from talking with a number of men is that no man *wants* to be a bad father. I doubt if any man ever says, "Okay, I've got a son now. I'm going to be the most terrible father I can possibly be, just to make his life miserable." Perhaps a very few men who have been hurt deeply by their fathers feel that way. But on the whole, I think every man would like to be a good father. We are just hobbled by whatever role model we may have had in life.

Forgiveness and understanding are the most important ingredients in the recipe for healing. Obviously, my relationship with the stepfather who raised me was never really very good. I always thought I learned how to be the kind of father I *didn't* want to be from him, instead of the one I wanted to be. But when I look back on the kind of father he had, I think maybe he did the best he could with a limited amount of skills and knowledge. While he and my mother did many things that I would have chosen to be done differently in my childhood, I've come to believe that he had no malicious intent in his fathering, merely ignorance tinged with apathy and possibly a pinch of panic. The fact that he grew up with my biological father in the backwoods of Wisconsin (not a haven of child-rearing education to begin with) and did not like my biological father as a boy contributed to his seeming contempt of me. Combine that with the fact that I look exactly like my biological father, and it's easier to understand his attitude. I also remember my stepfather's dad as a mean-spirited old man who ate Limburger cheese on hard rye crackers every night before bed. He did not appear to be interested in having a good relationship with his sons, and from stories I've heard of my stepfather's childhood, he never acted like he was either.

But the past doesn't have to shape our future. Dennis Rainey says it like this:

> Even if you were raised in an abusive situation, God gives the grace to honor trials. We can literally honor a mother or father who abused us by making a decision to value them. They don't have to earn it. I can almost guarantee you that they were abusive because they were abused as kids. Chances are, if you were abused, your grandfather abused your parent. The Bible says that the sins of the fathers are visited unto their children to the third and fourth generation (Exodus 34:7), so you could be suffering today because of a great-great-grandfather and blaming your parents for it instead of loving them and giving them honor, which is God's will for our lives. . . . You can take control of your life by starting to honor others. You can strengthen your marriage by honoring your wife. You can develop close friendships by choosing to honor other men.[3]

Placing myself in the shoes of my stepfather when he was a boy helped me to recognize the role model he grew up with as a father. Once I saw him as a peer, as just another man who struggled with sin and incompetence, I could more easily let go of some of the grievances I held against him. If we accept the fact that our role models growing up play a big part in what kind of fathers we are, then understanding why your father parented the way he did is imperative to your growth. Every man reading this book has caught himself doing or saying something his father did that he always swore to himself he would never, ever do. If you struggle with forgiveness, see your father for what he was—not malicious, but perhaps misguided.

Of course, many men out there have educated themselves to be much better fathers than their dads were, and the direct intervention of God in our lives obviously can change us into better fathers than we are capable of being on our own. Extending grace to your father (or mother) and resolving whatever issues remain between you not only enables you to develop as a father but gives your children a wonderful gift. Many men who struggled as fathers become treasures as grandfathers when they no longer have the pressure of providing for and raising a family. And grandfathers are very important in the lives and the development of young boys. Grandfathers, our culture devalues the importance of older people, but you are your grandchildren's father's father. If their father is big in their eyes, think how much more powerful the father of their father appears—the man who raised their dad! Grandfathers are able to pass along wisdom and lessons from a lifetime of learning while reinforcing a father's values.

One way to understand our fathers better is to understand the legacy they passed on to us. That makes it easier to resolve any issues you may still have between you. Think about ways you and your father are alike and several ways you are different from him. Consider the similarities, if they are positive traits, to be gifts from your father. Those ways that you are different, especially if they are negative, can be looked upon as an opportunity to break a cycle.

Next, go talk to your father. You need to talk to him before it's too late. I see so many men who grieve the fact that they never made peace with their fathers and now it's too late—they've passed on. You have to make the first move. It won't be easy, but nothing worthwhile in life ever is. If your father has not approached you about resolving your differences by now, chances are he never will. You are a grown man and the leader of your family. You're not the little boy who was afraid of his father anymore. Shake off your complacency, take a deep breath, and go seek him out. If my son (or daughter) had a grievance against me that was keeping us apart, I would want him to come to me—wouldn't you? Well, I'm betting your father does too. If we want to be forgiven by our children, we need to forgive.

Be persistent. He probably won't want to revisit painful subjects. Approach him with grace and seek common ground. What are some pleasant memories of your childhood together? Ask him about his childhood. Even if your grievances are justified, don't come at him with them right away. That's a no-win situation as it immediately puts him on the defensive. Remember, your father is just a man—imperfect like us all. He needs to hear that you care about him as much as you need to hear it from your father.

And if you've never heard your father say, "I love you," you need to ask him. Otherwise, you will likely never hear those words. Many men, especially older men, had fathers who were raised in a generation that did not speak their emotions. It was considered

The Blessings of Being a Grandpa

In a classic study, researchers Bernice Neugarten and Krystyna Weinstein identified five benefits of being a grandfather:

1. **Biological renewal and continuity**: a chance to feel young again and a sense that your name, character, and family will extend beyond your lifetime
2. **Emotional self-fulfillment**: the sheer joy of being related to such adorable and talented grandchildren
3. **Being a resource person**: feeling useful through supplying advice, family history, and some financial support
4. **Vicarious achievement**: taking personal pride in a grandchild's performance or character
5. **Indulgence**: "spoiling" the children is a hoot! And it's a pleasure they may have denied themselves as parents.[4]

unmanly. But we have an inherent need to hear words of affection from our fathers. I remember how good it felt when I truly believed that God loved me. I finally had a dad who loved me—it was such a relief.

Even if you're stubborn like I am, you must realize that you need to mend fences with your father or father figure. I resisted for a long time approaching my stepfather to try to deepen our relationship. I confess I still have not been man enough to resolve our deepest issues yet.

As fathers we need other men to help us raise our sons—even though we don't like to admit it. It's in our son's best interest to have a grandfather help guide him through life. Other men also play a pivotal role. But oftentimes, because of pride, we must resist the urge to be the only significant male in his life.

The legacy you leave as a man is impacted by your heritage and specifically by your relationship with your father. If you do all that you can to resolve whatever issues are between you and your father and still fail, at the very least you will have no regrets later in life. You will also have done your best to fulfill God's commandment to honor your father.

And always remember, no matter what your earthly father was like or what he did to you, you *do* have a father who loves you—your heavenly Father. In fact, he loves you so much that he sacrificed his only Son's life for you. Would you purposely allow someone to kill your son if you knew your sacrifice would save other people—especially people who hated you? I wouldn't. But that's exactly what God did for you. God loves you just the way you are, with all your faults and imperfections. After all, he created you. He's more than willing to forgive you for every sinful thing you've ever done—no matter how horrible it was in your eyes.

God created us in his image to have *abundant* life. But he did not make us robots to automatically love and obey him. He gave us free will. All of us have chosen to disobey him and go our own willful way. God is perfect (holy), and we are flawed (sinful), and the consequence is eternal separation from God (hell). No matter how much we do or how good we are, we cannot be perfect. Perfection cannot exist in the same sphere as imperfection. Sinlessness cannot be allowed to be corrupted by sin—or it would become sin itself. It would be like putting a drop of nasty, grimy waste oil in a flask of pure, crystal-clear water. The oil would contaminate the entire flask of water.

But God took on himself the penalty his holiness demanded for our sin. Jesus, God the Son, died a horrendous death on the cross in our place, bridging the gap between God and people. He died so that we do not have to die. So we must accept his gift of sacrifice in order to have a personal relationship with God.

Your relationship with this Father is too important to ignore. If you haven't already done so, I urge you to ask your heavenly Father to become part of your life. You can do it right now. Just set this book down, close your eyes, and quietly say, "Heavenly Father, please forgive me for my sins. I accept the gift of salvation paid for by the death of Jesus Christ, your Son. Please come into my heart and take control of my life. Amen."

It is not a complex decision, but it's still not always an easy one. And it's often not without pain. It requires setting aside your pride and demands honesty before God, which can be a hard choice. Eventually you will realize that God forgives those sins for which you struggle to forgive yourself. Once you invite your heavenly Father into your heart, life becomes much clearer, as if looking through a pair of binoculars that are suddenly focused.

Of course, the greatest part of having a relationship with God is eternal life. He is a Father who will never, ever leave you or forsake you—especially in times of trouble. But why else is this relationship important to you as a man and a father? It's important because it gives you a foundation on which to securely build the rest of your life—a source of guidance for all the remaining decisions and values of your life. It also gives you a form of accountability like no other.

If you've just placed your faith in Christ, congratulations! You've made the most important decision of your life. You've just been hugged with loving arms to the chest of the perfect Daddy. Forever. Now, more than ever, you're ready to begin raising noble boys.

Questions for Reflection and Discussion

1. Do you have any unresolved issues you need to deal with in your relationship with your father? What about with your heavenly Father?
2. If so, what are some ways you can approach your father and try to resolve them? Develop a plan to approach him and talk about your relationship, and write it down on paper. Include what your relationship would ideally look like if it could be any way you wanted.
3. Discuss with the men in your group how they have reconciled with their fathers. Make a covenant to pray for each other as you approach your fathers for reconciliation.
4. If you just asked God to become part of your life, finding a Bible-believing church to become a part of is essential. Your walk with other godly men is imperative to your growth as a Christian.

4

Bonding with Your Boy

*Until you have a son of your own . . . you will never
know the joy, the love beyond feeling that resonates
in the heart of a father as he looks upon his son. You
will never know the sense of honor that makes a man
want to be more than he is and to pass something
good and hopeful into the hands of his son. And you
will never know the heartbreak of the fathers who
are haunted by the personal demons that keep them
from being the men they want their sons to be.*

Kent Nerburn, *Letters to My Son*

I NEARLY POPPED ALL the buttons off my shirt when my son
was born, I was so proud. I would have been happy to
have a healthy child of either gender. But deep in my heart
I was secretly delighted to have a male heir to pass along my
bloodline—especially the first time out of the chute!

Oh, the visions I had of his future potential! Would he be a major league baseball player or the head of a large corporation? Maybe he'd be a university professor. Heck, he might even be president of the United States! (It could happen.)

I carefully chose his name with the flexibility to fit either a professional athlete or a captain of industry. I played it over and over in my mind, savoring how it would sound as I pictured him shooting out a manly, powerful hand in a confident greeting: "Frank Johnson, pleased to meet you!"

Kind of silly, huh? But a man is mighty proud when his loins spawn a son to carry on his legacy.

But that's the easy part. Then begins the hard work of molding him into a man the rest of the world will look up to. And it can't happen with full effectiveness unless he bonds with you, his father.

Why Bond?

What's the big deal about bonding with our sons anyway? After all, most of our fathers, and their fathers before them, were never that concerned about this whole bonding issue.

They didn't make a big deal of it because it used to be built into life. Before the Industrial Revolution took men out of the home, fathers walked side by side with their sons just about twenty-four hours a day. That allowed father and son to bond simply as a natural result of living life. It also taught the son how to be a man through continual interaction with an adult male.

But most of us don't live on farms anymore. So why is it important these days that we bond with our sons?

By bonding with our sons, we are giving them life as men. Sons actively seek to form bonds with their fathers. They desperately need the nourishment or "father food" they get from dad. Your son was born with an incredible God-given urge to admire and worship his father. Why else are little boys always strutting around the playground saying things like, "My dad can whip your dad"? Why else do boys instinctively imitate their dads? I saw a little guy down the street the other day following along behind his dad as he mowed the lawn. The little tyke was pushing his toy lawnmower right behind in his father's footsteps, imitating every move.

A boy needs his father to show him how life is to be lived. He needs his father to show him what a man's responsibilities are and to pass on convictions that will guide him. In his father, he needs both a model and a teacher. A boy longs for his father. Kent Hughes says it this way:

> You have just finished a run, and you are sitting on the porch sweating like a horse and smelling like one, and your son, or perhaps a little neighbor boy, sits down next to you, leans against you, and says, "You smell good." This is the primal longing for one's father.[1]

Fathers are a necessity to their sons. Proverbs 17:6 says, "The glory of sons is their fathers" (NASB). The word *glory* in this text is a Hebrew word that literally means "weight." So we might read the verse, "The weightiness of sons is their fathers." A father who defines masculine boundaries for his son and paints a picture of healthy manhood gives his son weight or substance in life. Boys who don't receive this information become featherweights, lacking stability. They are easily blown away by any gust of cultural or peer pressure that comes along.[2]

Boys who have a physically or emotionally absent father are always trying to figure out life. They have no one to turn to for advice. This creates anger and frustration in a young man.

Preston Gillham says:

Men are a complex mix of extremes. Treat a man poorly if you are not close to his heart and he will shrug you off. But tread on his dreams and you wound him profoundly. Disrespect him from a distance and he pities you, but question his worth as one who has access to his soul and you possess the power to jeopardize his sense of identity. He is tough, resilient, driving, and independent, but molded through close, timely dependence upon his father and older mentors. Disturb his routine and he flexes. Disrupt the delicate transition from boyhood to manhood and he suffers immeasurably."[3]

Absent or Disconnected Fathers Can Create in Boys:

- Anger and pain (suppressed rage)
- Extreme behaviors, addictions, or obsessions
- Sense of lostness (indecisiveness, lack of direction)
- Homosexuality (sensitive boys are especially wounded deeply by the break with their father)[4]

By bonding with our sons, we help protect them from much of the suffering caused by the slurs and challenges the world slings at them. When a son bonds with his father, he finds a larger-than-life figure whom he instinctively looks up to, and having a hero provides courage for life's battles.

Kids picking on me at school? No problem, Dad will tell me how to handle it.

Girls acting weird around me? I'll get some advice from Dad.

Can't figure out how to solve a problem? I'll ask Dad.

If dad's there, everything will be okay in a boy's mind. Dad is an older male who loves him and encourages him no matter what the rest of the world thinks. When dad is not around, a boy is forced to face the harsh world alone with no one in his court to help shield or coach him; he's left without someone who understands his hurts, someone to commiserate with. A boy who lives within dad's protective sphere of influence finds a safe refuge where he can regroup, lick his wounds, and heal.

A father who affirms his children gives them the gift of confidence and self-esteem throughout life. It's part of the power that God has given men—power to lift others up or to destroy them.

Early in Jesus's ministry, he approached John the Baptist and asked to be baptized. Immediately upon emerging from the water, Jesus heard his heavenly Father say, "This is My beloved Son, in whom I am well pleased" (Matt. 3:17 NKJV). God was saying to him, "I'm proud of you, Son. Well done. Good job!" Clearly, God set an example here for all fathers of sons.

People grow, mature, and reach their potential as they are affirmed. People build much of their sense of self-worth based on affirmation or the lack of it. Sons get enough harassment and negative input from their peers and the culture at large. Fathers need to counteract that negative input, not add to it.[6]

> **What Every Boy Wants from His Dad**
>
> - Time together with dad—this creates experiences and memories
> - Direction from dad with solid "why" answers—not just "because I told you so" answers
> - Convictions that come from modeling (What do you *really* believe? What do we believe as a family?)
> - To see dad's heart (What's important in life to a man?)[5]

Everyone needs a cheering section. Your affirmation of your son counts for more than a stadium full of other people rooting for him.

Unfortunately, most of us have our hands full providing for our families, and this can easily keep us away from home for most waking hours of the day. Despite that obstacle, here are some ways I've discovered that we can form lasting bonds with our sons.

Physical Activities

Camping, hunting, fishing, sports, scouting, rafting, hiking, biking, climbing, church camps, and other outdoor activities all provide the physical outlet the male animal craves while allowing us to build strong father-son relationships. These types of experiences provide opportunities for fathers and sons to create memories that last a lifetime—memories that can be passed on from one generation to another. Another type of activity is a hobby that you both enjoy, such as collecting (stamps, coins, baseball cards, etc.), working on cars or small engines, wood or metal shop, attending sporting events, household maintenance, reading together, yard work and gardening, bird watching, miniature trains, model airplanes, wood carving, or just taking walks together. These are all great ways to bond.

I have a friend named Jim with whom I go hunting, hiking, and camping. Jim frequently pushes the envelope in his manly endeavors. More than once I've questioned my sanity while hanging off the side of some craggy cliff with him in the middle of nowhere. "We're making memories!" is Jim's favorite rejoinder. That doesn't always satisfy me at the time. But Jim's right. When all is said and done, at the end of our time on earth, we're left with the memories of a life well lived. Or not. And throughout their lives, our sons' most lasting memories are those of times spent with dad, often sharing in some physical activity.

Frank was eleven years old when we began hunting together with a group of men and their sons. I have always enjoyed the outdoors, and Frank had been a Boy Scout for several years. Consequently, both of us were experienced outdoorsmen and were familiar with guns, but neither of us had ever been hunting before. Oregon requires kids to go through a hunter's safety course in order to draw a tag for their first hunt at age twelve. So Frank tagged along to learn the ropes that first year. Little did he know, I didn't know the ropes myself. But my swollen masculine ego wouldn't allow me to admit to him that I didn't have a clue how to hunt deer.

After getting up at the crack of dawn three days running and never even seeing a buck, Frank and I were getting a little discouraged. We did see several does and were awestruck by the sudden appearance of a majestic, earthshaking herd of elk thundering down the mountainside a hundred yards away.

The eastern Oregon weather was unseasonably warm that October, and the third day was sunny with T-shirt temperatures as we headed out for a late afternoon hunt. My plan was to find a flat spot to lie down and take a nice, relaxing nap. Frank and I found a log beneath a copse of pine trees and sat down facing opposite directions. I was drowsing in the warm afternoon sun when I heard Frank urgently whisper with increasing intensity, "Buck, buck, buck! BUCK! BUCK!" I bolted awake. Turning, I spied a forked-horn slowly ambling across our field of vision about sixty yards downslope from our blind. As I sighted him in, he nimbly stepped behind a tree as if knowing he was being watched. I knew the big mule deer would bolt as he left the safety of the tree, so I aimed several yards to the other side. Suddenly, he leaped from behind the tree, bounding at a full gallop. As soon as he entered my sights, I fired. The buck neither stumbled nor broke stride as he continued up and over a knoll, out of sight.

Adrenaline rushed through my body. My pulse thundered in my ears. I spoke but then realized I couldn't hear my own voice because of the deafening roar of the rifle blast.

"I think I missed him. How could I have missed him at this close range?" I lamented.

"If it had been me shooting, you can bet I wouldn't have missed," Frank muttered, slightly disgusted.

As we searched the area where the buck had been for bloodstains or hair, Frank continued to chide me on my poor marksmanship. "I could've made that shot easy, Dad."

After searching for nearly a half hour and not finding any blood spots, I turned away in discouragement. But Frank refused to give up. His faith in his father remained intact, notwithstanding his criticism of my shooting.

Suddenly Frank shouted, "Dad! Blood!"

Sure enough, he'd found a small rock soaked with still-moist blood. At Frank's insistence, we combed the area in a grid pattern, looking for more stains. Every time we were just about to quit, Frank found another blood spot. After fifty yards or so, the stains grew bigger and closer together. As we crested a knoll, Frank yelled, "Dad! There he is!"

Sure enough, there was the buck, lying in a little depression where he'd finally stumbled and fallen. Being greenhorns, we hadn't realized that deer can run a significant distance even after being shot through the heart as ours had been.

As is usually the case, our walkie-talkie batteries decided this was a good time to give out. Unable to call for our more experienced compadres to come help gut and field dress the animal, it was up to us first-timers to complete the task by trial and error. Luckily, I'd been paying attention when the old "sourdough Bobs" had been explaining the procedure to another rookie back at camp the night before.

When our brother hunters did finally come upon us, we had the deer field dressed and nearly ready to transport back to camp. Blood up to our elbows, we basked in the glory of our friends' whooping praises and posed with our prize for the obligatory pictures. It was a scene that has played out countless times since the beginning of mankind.

Frank and I have hunted every year for the past seven years. Neither of us has bagged another buck during that time. But we sure look forward to hunting season every year.

About two months beforehand we both start getting antsy and checking our gear to make sure everything is in order. That first experience working together as a team—I the hunter, Frank the tracker—together overcoming trials we'd never experienced before, cemented our relationship for the rest of our lives. I look forward to sitting by the light of some future hunting campfire, spinning yarns to my grandson about the first big hunt for his dad and me. It was a time neither of us will ever forget.

Tough Times

Nothing draws men or boys together more closely than going through a difficult experience together. As we bear each other's burdens, we develop a bond that survives through life's future challenges. That's one of the advantages of performing physical activities together—stretching yourselves to attempt and conquer rigorous adventures.

Rest assured, life will sling its share of tough times at you. And when you stand side by side with your son during the trials and tribulations of childhood and adolescence, you develop a bond that helps protect him later in life. Realizing he has a dad who stands behind him gives your son the self-confidence to tackle seemingly insurmountable odds and attempt great things.

While being your son's advocate is vitally important, so is maintaining high expectations of him. Sometimes you need to set up challenges for your son. For instance, we have a huge backyard. At about age eleven, Frank was finally ready (and more than willing) to start mowing the lawn all alone. Suzanne, of course, was petrified that he was going to chop his foot off with the mower, but I let him stagger and stumble his way over the hilly terrain of our yard on his own. Not only that, but when he was finished, sweaty and exhausted, I made him go back out and redo the areas he'd missed as well as trim all the borders of the yard. I did this all under my wife's disapproving eye. At some point your son needs to be turned loose to accomplish certain tasks—like mowing the lawn, making household repairs, working on the car, or budgeting his allowance—all by himself. He needs to be challenged by being taught how to perform tasks that are difficult, then made to finish them and do them well. Being challenged and held accountable for these little tasks teaches him the skills needed to persevere through tougher situations later in life. Also, letting him work through difficult circumstances on his own—like making him work to pay for the window he broke throwing a baseball—teaches him to be responsible for his actions.

Sometimes this creates tension between you and your son. It would be much easier to let him be less than he's capable of being. But stay the course. When your son knows you have confidence in him, he will internalize the image you have of him—an image of a competent, hardworking young man. Your son has a God-given internal drive to make you proud of him.

"Every son wants to live up to his father's name—every son wants to be so solid, courageous, tender, and capable that his father, beyond all others, will say of him, 'You've lived up to our name, son. I'm proud of you.'"[7]

John Maxwell says it like this: "Only when we are tested under pressure do we discover the true nature and depth of our character. By never letting our sons suffer through tough times, we rob him of the joy and rewards of developing strong character. People can *say* anything they want about their values, but when the pressure is on, they discover what their values really are."[8]

That's why resisting the urge to rescue our sons all the time is important. A fine line exists between being supportive and enabling. Your son needs to learn early on to be accountable for his actions—accountable not only to you but to the world at large. His decisions as a man will have far-ranging ramifications. He needs to know that while you are always his dad and will be there for him, he will also be subject to the consequences of his decisions. The sooner he learns that lesson, the easier life will become.

I've learned to value the lessons God teaches me through trials. Had I been "rescued" from hardships by a rich daddy or allowed to succeed to the socioeconomic level I desired, I might never have been open to following God's will for me. God used tough experiences to train me to be a good steward of the ministry gifts he has given me.

As God's representative on earth, you can help your son learn these lessons early in life, and perhaps God will not find him quite as hardheaded as I have been.

Ceremonies

As boys progress through life, they need ceremonies in order to know when they have become men. Many men never know when this transition has happened. I certainly didn't. Even after I had fathered a child, I wasn't sure what made a boy a man. Was it the first time you drank a beer? Maybe when you graduated from college or bought your first car? What about sex—is that what makes you a man? Your son will go through the same confusion if you don't prepare him for his graduation into manhood.

Our culture has done away with many of the ceremonies that used to indicate when a boy became a man. These were signs to let the boy and everyone else know, *This young buck is on the road to manhood now. It's time to put away childish ways. It's time to start treating him differently and to have higher expectations of him.*

When my son, Frank, entered adolescence, I initiated a small ceremony to mark the occasion. He and I went to dinner at a nice restaurant. During dinner I discussed with him some of the challenges he would face in the next few years—physical changes his body would undergo, peer pressures he'd face, sexual urges he'd feel, and the confusion girls would present. I then prayed for him and gave him a purity ring to remind him of our discussion. This ceremony marked the beginning of his journey into manhood.

As Frank approached graduation from high school, I was determined to do something significant that would impact his life. About six months before his graduation, I began planning a dinner. I asked a group of spiritually mature and deeply devoted men to pray about what advice God would have them impart to a young man on the cusp of manhood. I prayed daily for God to put his blessing on this occasion and to give me the wisdom to prepare an event that would honor both God and my son.

When we met for dinner that night, the ceremony affected not only my son but also every man in attendance. Each man spoke on subjects that God had placed on his heart. They gave Frank advice, spoke of their own mistakes and regrets, and shared from their own experiences about what they felt was important in a man's life. Some men spoke about the importance of friendship, some about the importance of God in their lives, and some about the devastating effects that pornography or abortion had wreaked on their souls.

Then I spoke. I told Frank that our relationship was now changing, that I would become more of a coach instead of an authority figure in his life, and that we were gradually becoming peers. We recorded the event on videotape so Frank can look back from time to time at the priceless advice he got from those men.

I intend to have a similar ceremony just before his wedding day, when a group of mature, wise men who have each been married for a lengthy period of time can give him their advice on marriage. (I'll be taking notes as well.)

The benefits of these milestones and ceremonies in a boy's life are easy to understand. But what happens when young men are not provided with some sort of ritual to initiate them into manhood?

Michael Gurian says, "When a male is not provided with rites of passage to mark each of his transitions through adolescence, we can expect him to create rites of passage of his own."[9] Often these rites of passage might include smoking cigarettes, having premarital sex, committing vandalism, or any number of other unhealthy activities to show himself and others that he's becoming a man. When men don't show boys what it means to be a man, the boys make up their own rules and ceremonies. A gang is merely a group of boys searching for their identity as men. The younger members look to older boys, and usually none of them have ever had men in their lives to provide wisdom and be role models. These boys create bizarre, dangerous, and destructive rituals in their quest to prove their manliness.

Ceremonies not only mark the stages for your son as he progresses toward manhood but also provide a great vehicle for you to bond with your boy. Make these ceremonies memorable. This requires planning, creativity, and maybe even some expenditure on your part. Most of all, it requires your time. Time is the most valuable commodity you can give your son. It is more precious than any other gift, material or otherwise, that you can give him. Look for opportunities to initiate your son into manhood so that someday he will not have to ask other men, or even his wife, "Am I a man yet?"

One Man's Journey to Manhood

Here's a story that illustrates the power of men initiating boys into the fraternity of men. Just their very presence together represents a sort of mysterious rite of passage. This is a portion of a wonderful article by Bryce Towsley called "Deer Camp Dreaming":

> Back in the Pleistocene era of the 1960s, before enlightenment brought its many changes, Vermont deer camps were a man's domain. No ladies, no babies and no apologies. This was a masculine world filled with a smoky haze, hard drinks, high testosterone, harsh language and rough jokes. It was a place where a man could cut loose, revert to a hairier time and act as all men must from time to time, and I longed to be a part of it so much I thought I would burst.
>
> But, to my eternal anguish, the rule at "Camp Buckless" was that you must be at least sixteen years old and I was several years short of that. Even back then I was hard to ignore, and by the time I was twelve there was a little rule bending and I was allowed day visits. I used the time to lobby hard for the rules to be further relaxed. I don't know how many floors I swept or how many times I loaded the wood stove, but with some coaxing from my Uncle Butch the long standing rule was waived for me, the first of my generation, and I started to hunt from the family deer camp in my thirteenth year.
>
> It's been thirty-six years, but I remember every detail, how in awe of it all I was. Even today I can still recall the smell of the camp, a mix of old wood, wet wool, cooking meat and a blend of tobacco and wood smoke stirred with a thousand other odors that can only be identified as "camp" smells, until they melded into something unique to that place and time. At night I

*would sit concentrating hard so that I could remember
everything. I would be perched on the ladder (for it's
much too steep to be realistically called stairs) to the
loft and looking down at this group of men that I knew
so well, yet who now seemed so strange. I remember
listening so carefully to the stories my grandfather and
the others were telling of the glories of past hunts, and
to the rough jokes that my young mind understood only
to the extent that somehow I knew by hearing them, I
had taken the first step to being accepted as one of the
men.*

*I recall the strange and powerful longing that was
threatening to devour my guts, a longing to belong to
this group, to fit in. I knew that my invited presence was
a sign that I was on the road to that acceptance, but I
didn't really have a clue how I could tell when I finally
got there. I am sure that even when I am very old and
my life is behind me, it will still be fresh in my mind
how I reveled in that first weekend in camp and how I
tried so hard to please, to fit in, to be one of the guys,
all the while knowing in my heart that I was failing. I
can still feel the anxiety and the terrorizing knowledge
that I would never get it right. How could I know that
only time could make it work? I was thirteen, what did I
know about time?*

*I remember so well the excitement of that first night
and how the camp seemed to have a life of its own,
one fed by the power of these men, a power too strong
to be contained. In my youth, I could sense it, but it
puzzled me. It was, I now understand, the power of
anticipation. An anticipation that only can be generated
in the waning hours before the deer season opened. That
anticipation fueled an excitement that permeated the
camp until it filled the available space, overwhelming
everybody there, and I knew that no one in that room
would ever again have friends as good or as close as
those who were with them at the moment.*

69

I can still taste the huge "grownup" breakfast my Uncle Bud cooked the next morning and the bitterness of the coffee as it scalded my taste buds for the first time in my young life. Old injuries and years of shooting have ruined my eardrums, but even today I can clearly hear the squeak of the snow as we left the camp in the dark and I remember vividly the stark contrast of the cold and clean northern air to the humid and smoky interior of the camp and the chill that went through me when we stepped out the door. It's so easy to venture back to that morning on the edge of the hardwoods with my back against a big maple tree, sitting and shivering, but not entirely from the cold. I can feel the cold steel and the dark stained wood of the old 1892 Winchester that Gramp had loaned to me amid solemn vows and sworn oaths to treat it like it was the most delicate treasure on earth, because in my mind it truly was. I can smell my father's unfiltered Pall Malls mixing with the sharp chemical odor rising from my own freshly dry-cleaned wool coat and see the glow as he smoked beside me in the dark.

There were days of hunting before that one and by then I already had a couple of deer to my credit, but I don't think there was ever a day that made a more enduring impression. That I was finally hunting from the deer camp made all the difference. There have been many deer hunts in the years between that day and today, and most have faded from memory. That morning, though, remains as vivid as it was in 1968. I remember how boredom replaced excitement as the day played out, but that it didn't seem to matter. I recall too how things that are now vexing or at least mundane were pure excitement and how the newness of all the experiences threatened to overwhelm me.

The camp was deep in the woods at the end of miles of bad road, a road rutted deep with mud and mined with ledges and hidden boulders. That night, we hit a

*rock that hung the snow-plow frame on the old Jeep
and in spite of chains on all four wheels, we were stuck.
To the others in the truck it was a reason for more bad
language and foul tempers, but for me it was grand
adventure. Later as we pulled into the camp yard, the
dim, mud-crusted headlights swept quickly across a
bear that was hanging from the meat pole. That quick,
unexpected glimpse scared me breathless. But at the
same time, deep down, it excited me. It was true! There
were bears lurking in these woods we were hunting! The
element of danger, adventure and excitement stirred by
that knowledge generated in my young soul a thirst for
it all that was beyond measure and unquenchable even
today. That evening, as I sat in my "stand" listening to
the story of the bear, I barely dared to breathe, afraid I
might miss a syllable.*

*In the following weeks and years I spent many happy
hours perched halfway up that ladder, and I am sure
that it was pivotal in my life's direction. Those days at
deer camp undoubtedly helped to lay the foundation for
my lifelong interest in shooting and hunting, an interest
that would evolve into my livelihood and in truth, my
life. Perched on that ladder I felt like I was part of
something big, something strange, exotic, mystifying and
oh, so desirable. I felt like a member of this glorious deer
hunting fraternity.*[10]

Give your son the gift of bonding together as you invite
him into the fraternity of men. Then launch him into the
world and see the difference he makes.

Questions for Reflection and Discussion

1. What kind of physical activities do you participate
   in with your son? Share with your study group some

"epic" memories of past adventures (practice your storytelling).
2. Describe a tough time you and your son have been through. How did it end up?
3. If you have a stepson, talk to the other men in your study group about ways you can bond more closely with him.
4. Think about some ceremonies that you can initiate for your son. Plan one (or more) out and then implement it at the proper time.

5

Mistakes All Dads Make

An expert is a man who has made all the mistakes
which can be made in a very narrow field.

Niels Bohr, quoted in Alan Mackay,
The Harvest of a Quiet Eye

IF THE QUOTATION above is true, I must be getting pretty close to being an expert father by now. As a matter of fact, the only reason you're holding this volume now is that I've made enough mistakes to fill up a book! Hopefully, though, I've learned from the mistakes I've made. The mark of a good leader and a good father is just that—the ability to learn from mistakes. The man who doesn't is doomed to repeat them over and over again.

I've said many times, "I wish I knew when my kids were little what I know now about fathering." Part of my being a more knowledgeable father just comes from having been a father for so long.

Becoming an effective leader takes time. We have to be seasoned; our experiences give us wisdom and humility. And the process takes time. Patience truly *is* a virtue, yet even developing patience takes time and practice. No man is a perfect father. I'm certainly not. We all fall short somewhere. The key is to take our strengths and nurture them while throwing off our weaknesses and replacing them with positive traits. But this often takes time and a lot of hard work.

Some weaknesses are designed into us by God. Some are conditioned into us by our upbringing. One of the toughest barriers I had to overcome as a father was the negative training I received as a boy. I had to forcibly train my mind to consciously reassess my reactions to people and difficult situations, replacing "instinct" with determined wisdom. It wasn't easy.

God created man in his image and endowed man with headship of his home. That gives men a special place in God's eyes as leaders of their families. As such, we have the responsibility to train our sons to be leaders of *their* families as well. Understanding the ways to succeed and some of the most common ways we blow it will help you rise to that task.

The following areas are mistakes I've either made or seen other men make. I list these not because I've perfected these areas but because I finally recognize them for the problem spots they really are. Think about these areas and how you can train your son to avoid making these mistakes with his family.

Mistake #1—Emphasizing Weaknesses, Not Strengths

As a father I have a tendency to focus on the things my son does wrong instead of the things he does right. But as a coach I tell my players to focus on their strengths, not their weaknesses. Help your son find his strengths—his gifts from God. Focus on those instead of being overly critical of his weaknesses.

Talk to your son about his God-given strengths and weaknesses. All of us have been blessed with certain skills and find ourselves lacking in others. Find out where your son excels, and help him use and cultivate those strengths to succeed in life.

When Frank was in elementary school, it became apparent that he probably would not become a star athlete. Not because he wasn't physically capable or coordinated enough—he played sports and did pretty well in all of them. But he did not seem to have the drive or competitive desire—the "fire in the belly"—to be really successful. Rather than force him to be a sports star (as was my initial inclination), I chose to focus on his strengths. Thankfully, I realized in time that I wanted him to focus on athletics because that was an area of strength for *me*, not for him.

> ## Determining Your Son's Strengths and Weaknesses
>
> 1. What things is he good at? What areas does he struggle in?
> 2. What does he enjoy or like to do? Is he passionate about anything in particular?
> 3. What is his temperament like? Calm, compliant, volatile?
> 4. What is his personality like? Is he introverted or extroverted?
> 5. What is his physical structure like? (Realize, however, that your son can change drastically as he grows. My son went from a scrawny little runt to a huge giant of a young man.)
> 6. What particular traits has God endowed your son with? Is he likable, compassionate, stubborn, strong-willed?

Frank is very intelligent, and he loves music. I encouraged him to join the band and learn a musical instrument. I told him, "You know, when I was in high school, I used to look up into the stands, and those guys in the band always seemed to be having such a good time. Plus, they get to hang around the cheerleaders and get excused from school to travel to all the games."

Whenever we watched college basketball or football games on television, I was quick to point out the camera shots of the band members cheering for their teams, many dressed crazily and with their faces painted. I also casually mentioned that the band members get into all the games free. Band members at a college that is a national powerhouse get to attend championship football and basketball games that most people never will.

Frank joined the band in sixth grade and has continued playing up into college. He has enjoyed himself immensely and has learned to play several instruments—a skill that will give him joy throughout his life. His positive experiences helped him develop a healthy self-esteem. If I had pushed him into sports, he might have struggled with his self-image. Instead of setting him up for failure, I helped him to succeed.

And yes, he got to hang out with the cheerleaders.

Mistake #2—Avoiding Physical Affection

As men we are raised to be uncomfortable with too much affection from another male—especially the physical kind. It's interesting that we compensate for that by knocking each other all around the football field, wrestling mat, or boxing ring. For some reason we think it's okay to slap another man on the butt during the heat of athletic competition, but we're uncomfortable hugging one another in greeting. As physical as the male animal is, you'd think we would be more comfortable expressing physical affection. But I think it must be a social taboo ingrained into our unconscious minds at an early age.

Hug and kiss your son. Give him plenty of physical love. Even as he gets older, continue to show him physical affection.

And in case you missed it, yes, I said kiss him. Sometimes it's uncomfortable for us grizzled old-timers, but it pays big relational dividends. I started early, when my son was a baby, showing him physical affection. It was easier at that time than it would have been later on. I made a decision when he was born that I would overcome my natural reluctance and show him the physical affection I had craved from my dad as a boy. That's a decision I have never regretted.

I smile now when I think of the times my son, even after entering adolescence, slipped his hand into mine as we walked across a parking lot together. My initial reaction was always to flinch, but I fought the urge to reject his advance, forcing myself to hold his hand as we walked into the store. Sometimes we got funny looks from people, but who cares what other people think? He's my boy. Long after everyone else has moved on, your relationship with your son and his family will bring you joy and contentment. Even now that he's in college, Frank still comes up and kisses me on the forehead whenever he comes home or leaves the house.

When we are having rough times between us, I know that I can drape an arm across his shoulders or pat him on the back as a way of making amends and breaking the impasse of our disagreement. I still struggle with apologizing and asking forgiveness. But even if I can't verbalize or articulate my feelings to him, I know we can connect through a touch, all because we are comfortable in showing manly physical affection to each other.

Mistake #3—Giving Too Little Time

The *Encyclopaedia Britannica* devotes a half page to the accomplishments of Charles Francis Adams, the son of President John Quincy Adams. The younger Adams followed the political trail of his father and became a U.S. diplomat to Great Britain. The encyclopedia makes no mention of Charles's family, but Charles's diary does. One day's entry reads: "Went fishing with my son today—a day wasted." Someone else's diary, however, offers a different perspective on that same event: "Went fishing with my father—the most wonderful day of my life." The person who wrote those words was Charles's son Brook. Interesting, isn't it, how a little boy's perspective can be so different from his dad's?

It's almost a cliché to quote the song by Harry Chapin, "Cat's in the Cradle," to illustrate the consequences of a father being too absorbed in his work when his son is young. The reality is that most of us men are taught by our culture that in order to be a success in life, we must be successful in our work—that our career is more important than anything else in life. Oh, we give lip service to the importance of our families, but our actions often speak louder than our words.

A mother and her young son were looking through an old family photo album when the boy noticed a snapshot of a handsome young man with dark, curly hair.

"Who's that?" he asked.

"That's your father," his mother replied proudly.

"Oh yeah?" said the boy. "Then who's that bald guy who lives with us?"

Maybe that father has been spending too much time at work and not enough time with his family.

One of the things I miss the most now that our children are older is having them run headlong to me yelling, "Daddy's home! Daddy's home!" when I walked through the door from work. As I look back I find that shuffling along with those little monkeys wrapped around each of my legs was an exquisite pleasure that I miss dearly. Their unbridled joy at seeing dad was more precious than silver and gold to my heart. Unfortunately, at the time I was more concerned with getting ahead, making my mark in the world, and providing for my family than I was with relishing those moments. Consequently, I often ran the kids off before they could fully express their joy at seeing me after a long day's absence.

As an experienced "older man," let me give you younger fathers a little advice. That season comes around once in life, and it is fleeting. If I could do anything over again, I would do a better job of decompressing *before* I got home from work so I could enjoy rolling around on the floor for a few minutes with the little rugrats. Now, with teenagers in the house, it seems as though no one cares when the old man comes home anymore—that is, unless they need money.

A man came home from work late again, tired and irritated, to find his five-year-old son waiting for him at the door. "Daddy, may I ask you a question?"

"Yeah, sure, what is it?" replied the man.

"Daddy, how much money do you make an hour?"

"That's none of your business! What makes you ask such a thing?" the man said angrily.

"I just want to know. Please tell me, how much do you make an hour?" pleaded the little boy.

"If you must know, I make twenty dollars an hour."

"Oh," the little boy replied, head bowed. Looking up, he said, "Daddy, may I borrow ten dollars, please?"

The father was furious. "If the only reason you wanted to know how much money I make is so you can borrow some to buy a silly toy or some other nonsense, then you march yourself straight to your room and go to bed. Think about why you're being so selfish. I work long, hard hours every day and don't have time for such childish games."

The little boy quietly went to his room and shut the door. The man sat down and started to get even madder about the little boy's questioning. How dare he ask such questions only to get some money!

After an hour or so, the man had calmed down and started to think he might have been a little hard on his son. Maybe he really needed to buy something with that ten dollars, and he really didn't ask for money very often. The man went to the door of the little boy's room and opened the door. "Are you asleep, son?" he asked.

"No, Daddy, I'm awake," replied the boy.

"I've been thinking, maybe I was too hard on you earlier," said the man. "It's been a long day, and I took my aggravation out on you. Here's that ten dollars you asked for."

The little boy sat straight up, beaming. "Oh, thank you, Daddy!" he yelled. Then, reaching under his pillow, he pulled out some more crumpled-up bills. The man, seeing that the boy already had money, started to get angry again. The little boy slowly counted out his money, then looked up at the man.

"Why did you want more money if you already had some?" the father grumbled.

"Because I didn't have enough, but now I do," the little boy replied. "Daddy, I have twenty dollars now. Can I buy an hour of your time?"[1]

Your kids aren't impressed with all your accomplishments. The only thing that really impresses them is your time and attention. Not spending enough time with our kids creates anger in them. There's really no greater insult than being ignored.

To realize that our kids love us, they want to respect us, and they want a relationship with us is a wonderful thing. "They just may be the only people in the world who *want* to love you, who *want* to respect you. With everyone else you have to *work* for those things. When we come to our kids and apologize, they want to repair the relationship with us. But when we refuse to humble ourselves, when we break our promises, when we publicly embarrass them or compare them or abuse them or ignore them, then anger begins to sour their souls."[2]

Think about that for a minute. Just by the virtue of who you are, and for no other reason, your kids *want* to love you. What a gift from God! It doesn't matter whether you're rich or poor or what you've accomplished. Just because you're you, they *want* to love and respect you. Even kids whose dads are in prison or are terrible role models still want to love and respect their fathers. Only after years and years of disappointment do they lose that feeling. (Actually, I don't think they ever lose it; they just guard their hearts to shield themselves from the pain.)

Your kids want to respect you. Yet sometimes we thoughtlessly trample on that gift. I know I have. God gives us that gift, and the only way we ever lose it is by our own actions and words. Only we can take away that instinctual desire that God places in our kids' hearts—no one else can. No one else could talk it out of our kids or even beat it out of them. That's the one thing they will hang on to more tightly than anything else.

The most wonderful thing about the gift of a child's respect is that even if we do trample on it, when we come to our children with a humble and repentant heart and ask for their forgiveness, the gift can often be reborn in them. It is never too late to seek the love of your kids.

Don't let your life get in the way of your family. Especially when the kids are young, men feel compelled to immerse themselves in work in order to get ahead and be successful in life. Even later on, some of us are still driven toward success and accomplishments that are well beyond our needs. Sometimes the reason for being driven is one of two things: either we are subconsciously trying to get the approval from our fathers that we never got as a boy, or we are angry at him and want to "show" him he was wrong about us—that we are worthwhile. Don't let those unresolved issues drive a wedge between you and the kind of father you want to be to your kids.

Time is the most valuable, and the most limited, resource we have to give to our children. Your son needs your time more than he needs your money.

Mistake #4—Pushing for Performance

I have a tendency to too often judge my children's efforts by their performance. The reality is that an individual can do his personal best in an area in which he is not gifted and still fall short of average performance. Likewise, a person who is gifted in an area can do well while applying very little effort. Which scenario should be applauded more? I think it's more important for your son's heart to be in the right place—for him to do things for the right reasons—than for him to be judged by the results of his efforts or performance. Sometimes I try to force my kids to behave a certain way by laying down the law instead of steering their behavior by changing the direction and focus of their hearts. As adults, our image of God is strongly influenced by the image we have of our earthly father. When we are overly critical or too strong as disciplinarians, we project to our children the image of a God who judges them on their performance. Instead, we should let our example teach them about his grace. By changing their hearts, we can make them *want* to change their behavior instead of forcing them to change through submission to our authority.

As men we often judge ourselves (and others) through comparison. We compare our achievements to see how we measure up. Unfortunately, we usually measure performance against the best, almost never with realistic expectations. We then wonder why we can't stack up against the professional athlete, the rich business magnate, or the man married to the supermodel. And we compare our sons against his best-performing peers as well. It's not very fair to us, and it's certainly not fair to your son to hold him up to such unattainable standards.

You can have high expectations for your son and exhort him to do his best. Remember, however, that mistakes are opportunities to coach your son, not to criticize him. In my experience, everything will work out just fine after that.

Mistake #5—Forgetting to Have Fun

We so easily get caught up in the complexities and stresses of everyday life. This is especially true for those who take responsibilities seriously. But part of a dad's charm is his ability to have fun. Let yourself go and remember all the goofy things that make life worth living. Have fun with your son while he's still a boy. Take some time to just goof off. You'll have plenty of time to be serious and somber. One of the things kids appreciate most about their father is his sense of humor. When dad has life under control, he values the humorous side of life and shows it to his kids.

Even the way a man plays with a young child helps develop specific portions of the child's brain. With his roughhousing behavior, such as tossing his child in the air, a man signals that it is safe to take risks—provided, of course, he catches the child before he hits the ground. Men who play with their small children help develop fundamental portions of the children's brains, giving them greater confidence and the ability to take risks throughout life.

The child, especially a boy, learns that risk-taking can be fun, rewarding, and sometimes dangerous. Good-natured wrestling with dad or other males also promotes physical development, emotional well-being, and self-esteem.

Remember how much fun it was to go to the dump with your dad? How about to carnivals, rock quarries, construction sites, and shooting galleries? The fondest memories I have of my childhood are when my stepfather let his hair down and acted goofy. All of us kids laughed ourselves stupid whenever he told funny stories or danced a silly jig. Sometimes he'd allow my sisters to put curlers in his hair to create a ridiculous hairdo. He once challenged me to a footrace around the block at three o'clock in the morning.

When my kids were little, we played "ride 'em horsey," with each child taking turns wearing out my knees riding me around the house. Our special game was "pin the bear." Both kids ran full speed and leaped onto me, trying to wear me out and pin the bear to the ground. The battle would rage back and forth until little Kelsey, finally pinned by the bear and abandoned by her brother, would holler, "Hep me! . . . Hep me!" as the bear growled and nuzzled her neck with his whiskers.

Humor seems to compensate for a lot of foibles. Besides, a dad needs humor just to survive some of the potholes along the road of fatherhood.

Mistake #6—Fearing Failure

I spent much of my life avoiding anything I wasn't perfect at because I was afraid to fail. This has caused me to have a number of regrets. There are two kinds of pain—the pain of discipline weighs pounds, but the pain of regret weighs tons. The regrets I have in life are mostly of things I didn't do, not of things I did do. Oh, I regret some things I've done over the years (I've done many things I'm not proud of), but I don't regret my sins of commission like I do my sins of omission. Missing opportunities, having an apathetic attitude, and not searching for significance were all choices I made that I regret deeply. I was raised to believe that failure is the worst thing of all. But it's not. I've come to understand that true failure is never reaching out to attempt something great, to try to reach your full potential. You only fail when you don't try.

This may sound strange, but I guess I regret never failing. Some people would feel proud of that, but never failing means you're never really doing anything. I believe in basketball coach John Wooden's philosophy that the team that makes the most mistakes will win the game. If my team is not making mistakes, it's because they are not trying very hard; they are not doing anything but standing around watching the action. They are not actively participating. The same can be said about life.

I regret all the times I was impatient with my children and didn't give them the attention they deserved. I've told Frank many times that he needs to know that whatever mistakes I made as a dad—and I made many—those mistakes were my problem; they never had anything to do with him. He deserved more love and better fathering than I was capable of giving him. I also told him that if I were ever to hear him speak to his kids like I'd spoken to him in the past, it would break my heart because I would know where those hurtful words had come from.

You have the power to hurt or help people's lives; treat it with respect. It's almost like having a superpower: it can be very destructive, so you must always use it for good.

I think about Samson, who was marked by God for greatness yet settled for just being a strong guy (see Judges 13–16). I think all men have been marked by God for greatness, yet the best of us just settle for being strong or better than average. Coach Wooden said, "Do not permit what you cannot do to interfere with what you can do."[3]

Think about what God created you for—what gifts did he give you? Then look for opportunities to use those gifts for his glory. Don't be afraid to fail.

Mistake #7—Abusing Your Power

Several years ago, during a rare bout of brutal self-honesty, I discovered that I treated my employees better than I treated my wife and children. I heard myself saying things to my family I would never say to my employees. If another man had made those kinds of statements to my wife or kids, I would have physically confronted him. Why did I feel free to verbally wound those I treasure more than anything else in the world with words that I would never dream of saying to a stranger?

The greater your love for someone, the greater your capacity to experience a wide range of emotions toward him or her—*including* the harmful emotions of irritation, resentment, anger, and rage.[4] Often these are transferred emotions. We're really mad at something or someone else, or even ourselves, but our family is a "safe" entity to dump our anger on.

When we exhibit wrathful behavior, we lose our effectiveness as leaders of our homes. We have to remember our place as God's representatives in leading our families.

John Emerich Edward Dalberg said, "Power tends to corrupt, and absolute power corrupts absolutely."[5] As fathers we pretty much have absolute power within our homes. We must take care not to become corrupted, allowing that power to bring out the worst in us.

Your position never gives you the right to command. It only imposes on you the duty of living your life so that others can receive your orders without being humiliated.[6]

Two verses from the Bible in particular remind us men to go easy on our sons. One is Ephesians 6:4, which says, "Fathers, do not exasperate your children; instead, bring them up in the training and instruction of the Lord." In other words, do not be unreasonably severe or ridicule your children. Colossians 3:21 says, "Fathers, do not embitter your children, or they will become discouraged." A father must be careful not to frustrate or discourage his children. Rules should be reasonable, not arbitrary. A father should train his children the same way God disciplines and teaches him.

When I think of the things I've said to my boy, when my tongue was like a double-edged sword, I realize I've been guilty at times of both discouraging and exasperating him.

One area in which I had to learn self-discipline was controlling my anger. I think more and deeper damage is done to relationships by anger than any other factor. Women and children are both severely affected by a man's wrath. When we fail to control our tempers, we do not model noble leadership skills to our sons.

Anger has a place, but it is rare. Commonplace, angry displays of temper are more often than not actually a substitute for a lack of leadership skills on the part of an insecure leader.[7]

Hugh O'Neill summarizes a man's repressed anger well: "I am absolutely sure that a lot of Daddy anger has more to do with unrealized dreams than with messy rooms. Trust me. You're not really angry at your kids. You're angry at somebody else, somebody who is a far less distinguished person than he dreamed of being."[8]

I think that sums up a lot of my anger as a young father. We'll talk more about anger control later on in this book in the chapter on discipline.

God has given us men great power that can be used for good or evil. Just look around at some of the problems men have created in other people's lives. Then look at some of the great things men have accomplished to benefit others. It's an awesome power. But with it comes the need to understand it and use it responsibly. Former United Nations Secretary General Dag Hammerskjöld said, "Only he deserves power who every day justifies it."[9]

A number of years ago I realized that I had gotten into the terrible habit of saying no every time one of my kids asked me something. This was clearly an abuse of my power as a father. I often said no merely as a reflex reaction, even though later I realized I had no good reason for rejecting their request. I explained to my son and daughter that if I did not have time to properly process their request before they expected an answer, I would be more likely to decline it. Now they know to give me some time to process their request before expecting an answer.

Remember to be careful what you promise. Many times we say things or make commitments that we can't keep. These broken vows don't seem like a big deal to us, but they are huge to your son. Anything you say short of "no" is usually taken as a promise by your children. Be judicious about the promises you make. If you are not absolutely positive that you can keep them, do not make them. Your tongue has great power.

Many things in life, such as firearms or prescription drugs, have the power to be used for good or to be abused. You wouldn't take something of great power like a nuclear warhead and abuse it, would you? No, you'd respect the potential it has for devastation (although many men I know might be tempted to take it apart to see how it works). The same goes with the power God has put in you. Learn all you can about that power, and use it wisely. Then teach your son about the potential destructiveness with which men are endowed. Teach him to use power responsibly.

Mistake #8—Neglecting Your Need for Friendships

Most men in our country have many acquaintances but no real friends. The pressures and time constraints of work and supporting a family take away the opportunity to build masculine relationships. In order for your son to escape this trap, he needs male friendship modeled for him. Your boy needs your friendship as well as your guidance. To be the best father possible, you need other men in your life to hold you accountable and to lift you up during difficult times. Another man's experiences are invaluable when we try to navigate some of the uncharted waters of fathering.

When I became a Christian at age forty, I was one of those men with no friends. Hence, I was lonely—miserably lonely. Shortly thereafter, I acted on faith to start praying every day for God to bring friends into my life. Now, six years later, I find myself abundantly blessed with dozens of good friends and rich, full masculine relationships.

During his senior year in high school, Frank came home and told me about an incident that had happened in class. His current events teacher had remarked that men in our culture do not have friends anymore; they only have acquaintances. They do not have anyone they could call in the middle of the night for help. Frank said he thought to himself, *That's not true. My dad has many friends. I can think of at least a dozen men he could call in the middle of the night who would help him.* He was right! That's when I realized that God had truly blessed me by answering my earlier prayers for friends.

How did we men come to find ourselves with this isolationist mentality, and how do we go about changing it? Dr. Larry Crabb states,

> Men who as boys felt neglected by their dads often remain distant from their own children. The sins of fathers are passed on to children, often through the dynamic of self-protection.

It hurts to be neglected, and it creates questions about our value to others. So to avoid feeling the sting of further rejection, we refuse to give that part of ourselves we fear might once again be received with indifference. When our approach to life revolves around discipline, commitment, and knowledge but runs from feeling the hurt of unmet longings that come from a lack of deeper relationships, then our efforts to love will be marked more by required action than by liberating passion. We will be known as reliable, but not involved. Honest friends will report that they enjoy being with us, but have trouble feeling close. Even our best friends (including spouses) will feel guarded around us, a little tense and vaguely distant. It's not uncommon for Christian leaders to have no real friends.[10]

Does that sound familiar? We have to take risks in order to make, develop, and keep friendships. Maintaining a friendship is hard work. We have to reach out to other men whom we think we might be interested in befriending. Then we have to be vulnerable, opening ourselves up and allowing them to see our "inner man." That's not very easy for most of us.

In order to become an effective friend and leader, one must learn to be vulnerable with others and develop an ability to share feelings. It is a vital step to becoming a real person with whom others can connect emotionally. This is not easy to do if your parents did not teach you to share your emotional life with others. Emotional vulnerability is especially hard for men.[11]

One of the things I've discovered about making friends is that *we* have to be the ones to reach out and initiate friendship overtures. Often people reject these efforts, but instead of taking rejection personally, just understand that probably for a variety of reasons, now might not be a good time. I try to give people the benefit of the doubt as often as possible. I suspect most people either are overwhelmed with life or just don't know how to accept and develop a friendship anymore. My philosophy is to treat them with respect and openness, and if they don't reciprocate, then that's their problem, not mine. If they do show an interest in becoming friends, then we have to care about them, not just ourselves. We have to reach out and make the effort to find out their needs and try to help with them.

Your son needs friends, and so do you. He needs to see how a man relates to another man in a healthy relationship. He also needs to see you being voluntarily accountable to other men.

Isolation is death to a man's character. Perhaps that's why our culture, seemingly bent on the destruction of positive masculinity, continues to promote the rugged individualist as the model for men to look up to. The Marlboro Man, Dirty Harry, John Wayne, and James Bond—our celluloid heroes—never needed any help from other men. They just sucked it up and overcame whatever problems popped up. Then they rode off into the sunset by themselves.

But real men need other men. We need the accountability, comradeship, support, and yes (*gasp!*), help that other men can provide.

After all, if the devil can deceive a man, distract a man, separate him, and quarantine him from other men, the chances

What Scripture Says about Friendship

The Bible speaks many times about men needing friends and about the dangers of isolating ourselves. Here are just a few verses:

As iron sharpens iron,
so a man sharpens the countenance of his friend.

Proverbs 27:17 NKJV

A man who isolates himself seeks his own desire;
He rages against all wise judgment.

Proverbs 18:1 NKJV

In a multitude of counselors there is safety.

Proverbs 24:6 NKJV

If one falls down,
his friend can help him up.
But pity the man who falls
and has no one to help him up!
Also, if two lie down together, they will keep warm.
But how can one keep warm alone?
Though one may be overpowered, two can defend themselves.
A cord of three strands is not quickly broken.

Ecclesiastes 4:10–12

of isolation haunting his soul and creating masculine doubt are enhanced.[12] Masculine doubt is when we question our God-given roles as leaders in our homes and communities. And when masculine doubt is created, our leadership abilities are seriously eroded.

Every guy knows (or should know) that certain things, you just don't do alone. You don't go into the woods by yourself at night, you don't go swimming by yourself, you don't go hunting by yourself, and you don't go mountain climbing or out on the ocean by yourself. And if you're smart, you don't go through life by yourself either.

Even if you struggle with having good friends instead of just acquaintances, make sure your son understands the importance of friends. Help him see how you regret and have missed not having strong masculine friendships in your life. If you do have good male friends, make sure to build them up to your son often. When you are gone, he will need other men in his life to hold him accountable and lift him up.

Mistake #9—Being Inconsistent

Being consistent is one of the strongest traits a man can bring to fathering. Kids rely on you to be consistent in your responses no matter the circumstances. They rely on you to be dependable, a rock in the face of adversity. When life throws a curveball, they need dad to be there to tell them it's okay. Think about how scared you would be if the leader you were following—maybe someone you thought was strong or even invincible—were to suddenly become very frightened or to exhibit erratic, out-of-control behavior during a stressful situation. Would you want to follow that person again? I wouldn't. Your emotional stability, especially in stressful situations, provides your son with the security he needs in order to grow into a healthy man. You can't keep stressful situations from happening, but you can control how you react to them. Teach your son that a man keeps his head while others around him lose theirs.

Bill was the kind of dad who was never consistent in his responses to everyday situations. His kids never knew what to expect from him. One time he would react with humor, and the next time the same situation presented itself, it would provoke rage in him. This caused his children to be insecure, frightened, and lacking in self-confidence. Bill finally grasped the significance of being consistent during an incident with his son.

One day while Bill was fixing the lawnmower, the wrench slipped, and he busted his knuckles against the engine mount. Yelling out in anger, he swore and flung the wrench at the wall as hard as he could. Bobby, his five-year-old son, was entering the garage just as Bill threw the wrench toward the wall with the door. Seeing the impending disaster, Bill tried to reach out and take back his actions—"Bobby! No . . . !" The wrench crashed into the doorjamb next to Bobby's head, splintering the wood. Bobby fell backward with a look of horror on his face. As Bill rushed toward him in relief, Bobby scrambled to his feet and raced to his mother in terror. It was weeks before Bobby would even look at Bill, much less talk to him again.

When he finally would talk about the incident, Bobby said, "I thought you were just mad at me again. Sometimes you get mad and sometimes you laugh. I never know what I'm supposed to do. How come you don't like me, Daddy?"

Bill decided then and there to start controlling his emotions and become more consistent in his responses to stressful situations.

Mistake #10—Being Complacent and Passive

Several years ago my life was going along just fine. I attended church every week, read the Bible, and prayed daily. If you had asked me, I'd have told you I was probably at least as devout as most Christians. I felt pretty good about where I was spiritually, and certainly my family was much better off than they had been several years previous, before I became a Christian. My business was rolling along as usual. Nothing seemed out of the ordinary. In fact, I seemed to have finally attained some contentment in my life for a change.

One day I was reading my Bible. Have you ever noticed that some verses just leap out at you when you least expect it? This time Proverbs 1:32 leapt out at me: "And the complacency of fools will destroy them." I thought, *That's rather odd. Complacency doesn't seem like a thing to be destroyed over. It's not like murder or adultery.*

But this passage stayed on my mind for several hours, and I was finally compelled to look up the word *complacency* in the dictionary. Here's how it is defined: "self-satisfaction accompanied by unawareness of actual dangers or deficiencies."

When I put the verse and the definition together, I was thunderstruck. That was me! I was completely satisfied and totally unaware of any dangers in my life—dangers that were closing in all around me, threatening to destroy everything I'd worked for. Suddenly my heart started pounding and I got that sick feeling in my stomach. I realized that in my complacency, my business had been incurring financial debt and project losses, paying for them with credit lines over an extended period of time. In addition, a significant amount of employee lack of productivity that I had been ignoring suddenly became clear.

My first thought was, *My company is going to go out of business if I don't do something.* I hadn't realized until that moment that my then-ten-year-old company *was* literally teetering on bankruptcy. With some hard work, a good dose of humility, and a lot of cost-cutting measures, I managed to save my business.

But that passage didn't leave me. As I pondered it more and more, I asked myself, *Have I been complacent in my personal life and in the spiritual leadership of my family?* And I had to admit that I was contributing nothing to better other people's lives or further the kingdom of the Lord.

As I sought for God to show me how to stop being complacent in my life and in leading my family, I asked him, "But how can one man make a difference in this world? There are so many problems, it's just overwhelming." Eventually God confirmed to me that one person *can* make a difference in this world, but he has to start by doing something.

In order to break through the inertia of complacency, whether in our personal lives or as fathers, we must take action. And action requires courage and passion. So how do we find the bravery and fervor to take action? Jesus said, "Apart from me you can do nothing" (John 15:5). We must surrender ourselves to the Lord. Ask the Holy Spirit to fan the flames of passion in your soul and give you the courage to carry out the actions he would have you do.

For a significant period of time, I prayed consistently and passionately after the model of James 5:16: "The effective, fervent prayer of a righteous man avails much" (NKJV). I told the Lord that I was willing to follow him and that my life and family were his to do with as he would. *Please just show me what you want me to do*, I prayed. In response, God led me to start the Better Dads ministry, where I have the opportunity to impact the lives of men, women, and children. My wife and kids help out with the seminars and are much the better for the experience. And surprisingly, God led me to reevaluate my reasons for coaching basketball—something

I'd discovered that I had a passion for. Now I do it to impact teenagers' lives by teaching and being a mentor, not just for my own personal satisfaction.

Now how did this occur? Was it just coincidence? No, it occurred because I finally understood the warning about complacency in Proverbs. Complacency and passivity are man-killers in our culture. We need to consciously overcome these sappers of strength and be the men God has envisioned us to be.

Listen to what God says in the book of Zephaniah:

> And it shall come to pass at that time
> That I will search Jerusalem with lamps,
> And punish the men
> Who are settled in complacency,
> Who say in their heart,
> "The LORD will not do good,
> Nor will He do evil."
>
> Zephaniah 1:12 NKJV

Notice that God says he will "punish the *men*" [emphasis mine]. Not women and not children, but the men. He holds us accountable as leaders of our homes and communities. The last three lines of the passage sum up many Christians' belief that God will not take action either for or against them because of their passivity. Many people are lulled into complacency by the belief that God is apathetic and we will face no accountability for our inaction. This is precisely why we don't hesitate to break our marriage vows: we don't fear the wrath of God anymore.

In the movie *Schindler's List*, Liam Neeson stars as Oskar Schindler, a German industrialist during World War II. Never one to miss a chance to make money, Schindler marched into Poland on the heels of the SS after the Nazi invasion. He dove headfirst into the black market and the underworld and soon made friends with the local Gestapo bigwigs, softening them up with women, money, and illicit booze. His newfound connections helped him acquire a factory that he ran with the cheapest labor around—Jewish labor.

At first Schindler seemed like every other usurping German industrialist, driven by profit and unmoved by the means of his profiteering. But somewhere along the line, something changed. He succeeded in his quest for riches, but by the end of the war he had spent everything he made on keeping 1,300 Jewish men and women alive. He literally bought their lives.

In a powerful scene at the end of the movie, with Allied forces on the way, Schindler said good-bye to the many Jewish factory workers he had saved. As they gave him a gold ring in gratitude, Schindler broke down and began sobbing in remorse. He regretted that he had not done more to save additional lives. Even when his workers tried to assure him that he had done so much more than anyone else, he cried out in agony over his regret at his complacency.

Schindler, while certainly not as complacent as most others, realized too late that he could have done so much more. He regretted it dearly. And while others did not blame him, he knew in his heart that he could have done more.

I picture many of us, myself included, at the time of our judgment having the same repentant and sorrowful attitude before God that Schindler displayed in that powerful scene. It will be a time of grave recognition of missed opportunities and lost rewards.

Christians who are mired in complacency tend to think God is complacent as well. But God is never complacent. He is always active and passionate about his people, and he expects us to be as well. Some falsely believe that God will not correct their sin, so they are complacent about their own repentance. How can we not expect God to correct us? God will not be complacent. He *will* take some kind of action, even if that action is just being quiet until we learn patience or withholding financial blessings until we learn good stewardship.

So how do we take that first step out of complacency? Begin by praying to God and listening to his response. Pray to God for passion. Passion is the inner force that lifts a man out of the mainstream of mediocrity and into the lonely pursuit of his dream.

Ephesians 4:22–24 talks about spiritual growth coming from taking off the old, renewing the mind, and putting on the new. Here the apostle Paul compares the Christian life to stripping off the dirty clothes of a sinful past and putting on the snowy white robes of Christ's righteousness. In other words, once we understand the folly of complacency and God's judgment of it, we change our attitudes and willingly *want* to move beyond our belief into action. When we have put on the new (surrendered ourselves), God makes us able to hear the cries of the poor in spirit and empowers us to help them—maybe even our own children. He allows us to hear what he would have us do in his name and then to reach out and help others.

Teach your son the dangers of allowing complacency to creep into his life—both the spiritual dangers and the dangers to his manhood. I suspect too much time watching television and playing video games starts a boy down the path of complacency. Men mired in complacency and passivity are not noble leaders. They are, however, men with many regrets in life.

Questions for Reflection and Discussion

1. What do you consider the three biggest mistakes you've made as a father? What did you learn from them?

2. Develop a list of strengths and weaknesses your son possesses. How can you help nurture his strengths so he succeeds in life?
3. Chart the actual amount of time you spend each day with your son over a week's time. How does this amount of time differ from what you thought it would be?
4. In what ways would you like to overcome complacency in your life, both as a man and as a father? What types of failures do you fear, and how can you overcome the fear by taking the risk of failure?

6

Making a Noble Man

*Scripture's favorite description of a warrior is cap-
tured in the oft-repeated phrase "mighty men of
valor." Valor is a matter of character. Webster defines
valor as "strength of mind and spirit." It is this soul-
ish strength, this personal bravery, which "enables
a man to encounter danger with firmness." It is the
warrior's heart and soul which is the fountainhead of
courage, sacrifice, and unselfishness.*

Stu Weber, *Spirit Warrior*

O N THE FRIDAY following the September 11, 2001, ter-
rorist attacks against our country, I was scheduled to
have lunch with my good friend Jim. Jim is the pastor of a
small start-up church here in Oregon. As we stood in line to
order our food, Jim leaned over and whispered, "I'm going
to pray out loud at noon like President Bush requested."

Jim was really nervous and asked if I had any suggestions on how to go about this. I responded somewhat tritely but truthfully, "Nope. Better you than me."

As the noon hour approached, Jim stood up and said in a loud voice to the entire restaurant, "Could I have your attention, please? President Bush has asked the nation to pray for our country at noon today. I don't want to offend anyone, but we're going to be praying at our table, and I'd like to invite you to join us if you want."

A stunned silence greeted Jim's speech. Frankly, I admit, I was a little embarrassed. Jim sat down, and as we waited the five minutes for noon to arrive, no one came over. Just before we began to pray, a woman approached with her young son in tow and asked, "Could we join you? I think what you are doing is great."

At the appointed time Jim began to pray out loud. With my head bowed, I heard the scraping of one or two other people pulling up chairs around our table. Jim prayed out loud for our country, our president and other leaders, the emergency workers, our military personnel, and the families of the victims of the attacks. He prayed passionately from his heart. I estimate he prayed for about twenty minutes. During the whole time I did not hear any talking, music, or even doors opening and closing.

As he finished I opened my eyes and looked around. What I saw astounded me. The entire restaurant—perhaps twenty-five people, including the cooks and servers—were gathered around our table. Many had tears in their eyes. An entire restaurant had halted its operations during the busiest time of day. The owner came over with tears in her eyes and thanked us, saying, "You can pray here anytime you'd like."

Everyone had stopped what they were doing and come over to pray, all because of the courage and leadership of one man. It was one of the manliest displays I've ever seen.

Now whenever I say or hear Jim's name, this example of his leadership and courage will always come to mind.

I'm especially pleased that the young mother who first joined us brought her son. She showed much courage by being the first one to break the silence with action, thereby freeing up everyone else to act as well. Her son was blessed to have witnessed the courage displayed by both his mother and Jim.

Mighty Men

When we say someone's name, our mind instantly pictures that person. Different character traits that embody that individual also come to mind. When you think of what makes a good man, what character traits come to mind? How a man acts under stress tells a great deal about what kind of character he has.

Preston Gillham says, "The story of a man's life is the classic tale of a struggle between right and wrong, good and evil. He lives with constant tension, and how he conquers life and establishes himself proves if he truly understands masculinity or if he is misinformed about manhood."[1]

A certain school of thought encourages us to "speak it into existence." For instance, tell a man he's brave, and you help him become brave. With that in mind, tell your son all the things you want him to be: courageous, loyal, honest, strong, noble, and compassionate. Remind him of these qualities, and you help instill them within him. When he exhibits one of them, make sure to praise him. Point them out in others so he can see them in action. When you are fortunate enough to witness an example like the one Jim set, be sure to discuss it with your son.

Boys have a way of becoming what you encourage them to be. The Greek philosopher Heraclitus said, "A man's character is his fate." In the previous chapter we looked at some of the mistakes all men make. Now let's look at some of the character traits we need to instill in our sons to make their fate one of noble masculinity. Here are qualities that come to mind when I think of good men I know. Instill these qualities in your boy to help him become a noble man.

Perseverance

> Nothing in this world can take the place of persistence. Talent will not; nothing is more common than unsuccessful people with talent. Genius will not; unrewarded genius is almost a proverb. Education will not; the world is full of educated derelicts. Persistence and determination alone are omnipotent. The slogan "press on" has solved and always will solve the problems of the human race.
>
> Calvin Coolidge

The character trait of perseverance is fast becoming lost in our culture. Greatness is born by perseverance in the face of adversity. Few things worth doing are ever easy.

Marriages and families sometimes face hard times. Boys must learn to persevere in the face of adversity if they are to struggle forward later, during the even tougher seasons of life. Perseverance is probably one of the toughest things to teach boys. It requires us to resist the urge to rescue them when they are struggling. Letting them suffer goes against our nature, but suffer they must if they are to develop the strength for the long haul.

James 1:2–4 speaks of persevering during tough times: "Consider it pure joy, my brothers, whenever you face trials of many kinds, because you know that the testing of your faith develops perseverance. Perseverance must finish its work so that you may be mature and complete, not lacking anything."

Life isn't easy—it's not meant to be. Sometimes I feel like an old lion surrounded by a pack of hyenas, a once-mighty beast who's a little older, a little more tired, and a little slower. Every time I swat at one of the filthy, despicable scavengers, another is nipping at my rear end—all the while patiently stalking me and waiting for the opportunity to take me down for the final time. But I just keep getting back up.

When faced with the challenges and disappointments of life, we can respond in one of two ways. One way is to quit and blame someone else. People who do that end up with nothing in life. There's much truth in the saying, "Winners never quit, and quitters never win." Or we can look at setbacks as an opportunity to grow and improve ourselves—even as an opportunity to prove others wrong about us.

Strength does not quit. It finishes the task in spite of any difficulty, stays on course in spite of any hazard, and maintains pace in spite of any confrontation.[2]

When my son, Frank, was in sixth grade, he decided that he wanted to go out for the middle school wrestling team. I had wrestled all through high school, so I knew what he would be getting into. My son is a great kid, but he doesn't have a mean bone in his body.

After we discussed some of the harder aspects of wrestling, such as exercising vigorously, practicing constantly, watching your weight, and getting slammed to the floor repeatedly, he decided that he still wanted to try out. I have a firm rule with my kids: I don't care what they attempt, but they must stick with it for a reasonable amount of time, usually a season. So with that reminder in mind, Frank trundled off to the wrestling team.

Frank was heavy for his age, and since wrestlers are divided by weight classes, he naturally ended up wrestling eighth graders most of the time in practice. The difference in muscle mass between sixth- and eighth-grade boys can be huge. Many eighth graders have been through puberty and are developing man-like muscles—most sixth graders haven't. Two weeks into the season, Frank wanted to quit the team. He was getting hurt by the older boys in practice. He was coming home bruised and battered, crying and saying, "They are hurting me. I just don't want to be hurt anymore!" It broke my heart to look into Frank's teary eyes and tell him he couldn't quit. He was going to have to suck it up and be a man, to finish what he started. I prayed many times to God to confirm that I was doing the right thing.

To make matters worse, my wife was giving me "the look." You know the look. The one that says you've got a better than fifty-fifty chance of sleeping outside with the dog if this goes badly. That look. .

To make a long story short, I made Frank stay on the team. In his first wrestling contest, he was matched against a young fellow bigger than he was but about his age and maturity level. During the first two rounds and most of the third, Frank was tossed around the mat like a chew toy in the jaws of a puppy. His main strategy was to adopt a turtle-like posture on his belly—probably a defense mechanism learned from wrestling older and bigger boys in practice. Survival was his only goal. However, at the end of the match, his opponent, exhausted from pushing Frank's weight around the mat, inexplicably dropped and rolled over onto his back. Frank looked up in surprise, fell on top of him, and pinned him! Suddenly Frank's whole countenance changed. He jumped up, dancing around the ring on his toes with his arms in the air.

As he looked at me across the gym, he knew that the hours of hard work and pain had paid off. The reward was his because he had not quit when the going was tough. And the reward was that much sweeter—like cool, clear water refreshing his parched soul—because of the agonies he'd endured.

We soon discovered, however, we had created a monster. Frank went on to pin his next seven opponents before finally coming back down to earth. He never wrestled again after that season, but it provided him with several valuable lessons he'll remember his whole life—lessons such as hard work is its own reward, persistence and perseverance are rewarded, and you must finish what you start.

People today—men in particular—seem to quit more easily than they used to. They quit their jobs, they quit their marriages, they quit sports, they quit school, and they quit life whenever obstacles stand in their way or circumstances become too difficult. I've hired quite a number of young men straight out of college. They seem to believe that they are entitled to the same pay, working conditions, and job status as their fathers who have been in the workforce for twenty-five years. When that doesn't happen right away, they quit. In our era of instant gratification, the concept of "paying one's dues" has been lost in the rush to acquire as many material possessions as possible as quickly as possible.

James 1:12 says, "Blessed is the man who perseveres under trial, because when he has stood the test, he will receive the crown of life that God has promised to those who love him."

When we talk about persevering through tough times, we generally look at it from the perspective of someone else. It always seems tougher when we are the one going through the battle.

I have friends who have given up when the going got tough. These men, seemingly strong and manly on the outside, did not have the intestinal fortitude to keep fighting the good fight when the battles in their lives got fierce. They quit at the first twinge of pain. I shudder when I think of the examples they set in their sons' eyes.

I also have good friends who have struggled through failing businesses, daughters with eating disorders, marital problems, wayward children, cancer, and other illnesses. These men stayed the course and persevered during their times of struggle. They have come through their trials confident and strong in their faith. These men are an inspiration to me. Not surprisingly, each of these men's sons has a strong faith in God and a well-developed sense of perseverance.

Help your son understand the rewards that await him by overcoming and persevering through difficult circumstances. Character is forged in the furnace of affliction.

Perseverance is one of those qualities that build strength of character. And really, when it's all said and done, the only thing a man has that can't be taken from him is his character.

Mental Toughness and Resiliency

Sometimes life just knocks us flat on our backside. Out of the blue we get let go from a seemingly secure job, our wife leaves us unexpectedly for another man, or a serious illness sneaks up and jumps on our back. A man with mental toughness might get knocked down by these kinds of events, but like a modern-day gladiator, he refuses to stay down. He gets back up swinging.

Your boy is going to get knocked down from time to time. How he responds to adversity will dictate the resiliency he has within him. Resiliency is having the inner strength to cope with any challenge. It is crucial for any boy who's forced to face severe adversity. But in our fast-paced, stressful world, all kids need the capacity to overcome obstacles and deal with disappointments—whether in school, on the soccer field, or at the playground.

One of my favorite movies, *Rudy*, is based on a true story. The main character, Daniel "Rudy" Ruettiger, played by actor Sean Astin, is a young man from a blue-collar family with the dream of playing football for the University of Notre Dame. A student with poor grades and no money, he overcomes tremendous odds just getting accepted into Notre Dame. First he worked in a steel mill for four years to raise money. Then he attended Holy Cross College for two years to raise his grade point average high enough to meet Notre Dame's admission standards. On top of this, he had to work in order to pay tuition.

When faced with disappointment after disappointment, Rudy asked himself, *Have I done everything I possibly can?* Finally, after a long struggle and many disappointments, Rudy was accepted as a student at Notre Dame.

But being accepted to Notre Dame was only the beginning of his struggles. Being short, slow, and athletically challenged made making the football team seemingly impossible. As his boss told him, "You're five feet nothing and a hundred and nothing. And you've got hardly a speck of athletic ability." Only his attitude, courage, and persistence during tryouts gained him the admiration of a line coach, who gave him one of the precious few spots on the practice squad.

The practice squad ran the opposing team's plays each week against the first string. Rudy refused to allow the bigger players to stop crushing him in practice because he didn't want his weakness to hurt the team's chances of winning. Battered and bloodied, he sacrificed his all for the good of the team. After two years of allowing himself to be annihilated in practice by players much bigger, stronger, and faster than himself, he had earned the unconditional respect of every one of his teammates. Rudy's mental toughness had made up for his physical shortcomings.

Rudy's ultimate dream was for his father to see him on the playing field with the team during a game. None of his family believed he was really on the team because the practice squad did not "suit up" for games. Finally, at the insistence of all of the starting players, he was given a chance to suit up for the last game of the season his senior year. At the end of the game, with all the fans and his teammates chanting his name, he was even allowed into the game for the final play, and he tackled the opposing quarterback. He was subsequently carried off the field by the team to the wild cheers of the crowd.

Rudy's resiliency and positive attitude despite overwhelming odds impacted everyone who came in contact with him. His example of what we are capable of when we just don't quit should be an inspiration to all men and boys.

Resiliency is like a willow tree. During a fierce windstorm it bends but never breaks. It can also absorb devastating damage and bounce back healthier and stronger than before.

Some experts think resiliency is the most important character trait we can teach our children. Certainly, if you were to die early, resiliency would be the best character trait your children could possibly possess. It would allow them to go on and succeed in life in your absence.

Commitment

It takes a real man to be a father. Almost any adult male can perform a physical act and produce a child. But that doesn't make him a father. Being a father takes commitment. This is precisely why a dedicated stepfather is capable of being a better dad than an uninvolved biological father.

Several years ago, I was coaching the girls' JV basketball team at one of our local high schools. On trips for away games I made it my practice to sit at the front of the bus while the girls sat in the back. If you've ever been around a dozen sixteen-year-old girls, you understand—the noise can be deafening. One particular evening while returning home from a game, the bus was unusually quiet. As we entered town I heard a plaintive voice from the back exclaim, "There's where my daddy lives!" The longing and sadness in her voice broke my heart. Suddenly several other voices piped up, "My daddy lives at such-and-such address. Where does your daddy live?" Hearing these good girls long for their fathers brought tears to my eyes. I estimated from observations and comments I'd overheard during the season that about half of the team came from single-parent homes.

Remarkably, very few parents attended the games, and even fewer fathers showed up. These girls were nice, well mannered, and academically successful, yet each longed for the same thing—her daddy. I wish their fathers could have been on that bus and heard the anguished cries of their children's souls that night.

Another scenario occurred on my daughter's high school soccer team. My daughter and several other girls were sitting around after practice discussing their favorite topics—boys and shopping. As my daughter was bemoaning the fact that even though I supplied the money, I still went with her and monitored the kinds of clothes she bought, one of the girls stated sadly, "I'd give anything just to have my daddy around to go shopping with me." Several other girls readily agreed, causing my daughter to look at her shopping experiences in a whole new light.

Sociologist David Blankenhorn believes every man in the United States should be requested to take the following pledge:

Many people today believe that fathers are unnecessary. I believe the opposite. I pledge to live my life according to the principle that every child deserves a father; that marriage is the pathway to effective fatherhood; that part of being a good man means being a good father; and that America needs more good men.[3]

Being a husband and father takes commitment. Commitment is keeping the promises we've made, including implicit promises, such as when we commit to being a parent by simply becoming one. Your son will need this character trait when things get tough. Without it, he will let down those who depend upon him for their survival.

Integrity

A task becomes a duty from the moment you suspect it to be an essential part of that integrity which alone entitles a man to assume responsibility.

Dag Hammerskjöld, *Markings*

Integrity is doing the right thing no matter the circumstances. Integrity is not situational ethics. How can you teach your son to be an upright man of integrity in a deceitful and distrustful world? This story by Al Covino illustrates the kind of integrity I want my son to exhibit.

As a high school coach, I did all I could to help my boys win their games. I rooted as hard for victory as they did.

A dramatic incident, however, following a game in which I officiated as a referee, changed my perspective on victories and defeats. I was refereeing a league championship basketball game in New Rochelle, New York, between New Rochelle and Yonkers High.

112

New Rochelle was coached by Dan O'Brien, Yonkers by Les Beck. The gym was crowded to capacity, and the volume of noise made it impossible to hear. The game was well played and closely contested. Yonkers was leading by one point as I glanced at the clock and discovered there were but 30 seconds left to play.

Yonkers, in possession of the ball, passed off—shot—missed. New Rochelle recovered—pushed the ball up court—shot. The ball rolled tantalizingly around the rim and off. The fans shrieked.

New Rochelle, the home team, recovered the ball, and tapped it in for what looked like victory. The tumult was deafening. I glanced at the clock and saw that the game was over. I hadn't heard the final buzzer because of the noise. I checked with the other official, but he could not help me.

Still seeking help in this bedlam, I approached the time-keeper, a young man of 17 or so. He said, "Mr. Covino, the buzzer went off as the ball rolled off the rim, before the final tap-in was made."

I was in the unenviable position of having to tell Coach O'Brien the sad news. "Dan," I said, "time ran out before the final basket was tapped in. Yonkers won the game."

His face clouded over. The young timekeeper came up. He said, "I'm sorry, Dad. The time ran out before the final basket."

Suddenly, like the sun coming out from behind a cloud, Coach O'Brien's face lit up. He said, "That's okay, Joe. You did what you had to do. I'm proud of you."

Turning to me, he said, "Al, I want you to meet my son, Joe."

The two of them then walked off the court together, the coach's arm around his son's shoulder.[4]

That is precisely the kind of choice we need to reward our boys for making. Integrity like that is taught by the lifestyle we lead, the example we set as men.

One man I know spent a year in jail, losing his business, his house, and his life savings, because he refused to tell a judge that he would quit picketing an abortion clinic. He lost what the world says is important, all because he believed strongly enough in the biblical principle of "thou shalt not murder" that he was willing to stand by his values. That man's kids may have lost some material goods and some time with their father, but they have a dad they can look up to in legendary proportions. What an incredible example to set for your children. The legacy he leaves will impact generations. His heirs will be talking about what he did for many years to come.

Value what is right over what is popular. That provides a foundation upon which to build integrity and leadership skills.

Loyalty

As much as children need love from a dad, they also need a dad who is a loyal warrior, involved in the battles they face every day. During the Barcelona Olympics an unforgettable father-son scene occurred. You probably remember that moment when desperate failure was instantly transformed to high achievement by the love of a father.

Derek Redmond of Great Britain had trained for the Olympic 400-meter run for years. After the Seoul Olympics, he had a total of five operations on both Achilles tendons, but he bounced back. He was running well and competing in the Olympic semifinals.

Halfway around the track, however, Derek's right hamstring gave way. He fell to the track in agony, sprawled across the fifth lane.

The television cameras focused on defending Olympic champion Steve Lewis as he won the race and headed toward the tunnel. Medical attendants urged Derek to stay still, but he pushed them aside, struggled to his feet, and began hopping in a crazed attempt to finish the race.

Then something remarkable happened. Jim Redmond, Derek's father, witnessed his son's struggles from high up in the stands. Jim Redmond probably knew before anyone in the stands that something wasn't right. He also must have known that the best thing for his son's leg would be for him to sit down and get immediate treatment.

But this father also knew his son. He'd watched his son train for this moment for four years. His son had come to Barcelona for one reason: to finish this race. He knew how important that was to his son, and he was willing to do whatever it took to see his son achieve that goal.

Jim Redmond came rumbling out of the stands in his shorts and white T-shirt. All he knew was that his son needed help.

He flung a security guard out of his way and ran to his son, who was just reaching the homestretch. Jim Redmond put his arm around his son and said, "You don't have to do this."

"Yes, I do," said Derek.

"Well, then," said Jim, without hesitating, "we're going to finish this together."

The crowd realized that Derek Redmond was running the race of his life. They stood and cheered—just as I wanted to do as I fought back the tears when I saw it on television.

Derek leaned against his father, sometimes burying his face in his shoulder to hide his tears, and they stayed in Derek's lane all the way to the finish line. An usher attempted to intercede and escort Jim Redmond off the track, but his efforts were futile. They crossed the finish line, father and son, arm in arm.[5]

Jim Redmond was one loyal dad. How does one develop loyalty like that in a boy? You teach loyalty by being loyal. Does your son believe that you always have his best interests at heart—even when he's mad because you won't let him do what "everybody else is doing"? Does he know that you will stand by him even when everyone else is against him? Loyal dads produce loyal sons.

Loyal people stick with you when all else is in turmoil. Loyal people will still love you even when they know you. They are people who, despite your human failures, still believe in you. Those are the kind of people I want in my life.

My hope is that all fathers would have the loyalty to know their children and willingly spring into action to help meet their needs. We teach loyalty best by being loyal in times of struggle.

Manners

This is the final test of a gentleman: his respect for those who can be of no possible value to him.

William Lyon Phelps

Teach your son how to treat others. Politeness is just plain good manners, and good manners never go out of style. Manners show respect for others, regardless of their status or attitude.

Perhaps the best model to hold up to boys is the Boy Scouts credo, "On my honor I promise to be trustworthy, loyal, helpful, courteous, kind, obedient, cheerful, thrifty, brave, clean, and reverent." Not a bad model for a young man to aspire to, is it?

I believe that each of us has been blessed by God with individual gifts. Some people have the gift of athletic ability, some have been blessed with intellect, others are great orators or writers, and some are destined to be great leaders. In trying to determine what each of my children's God-given gifts are, I've come to realize that my son has been blessed with the gift of "likability." Everywhere we go, whatever situation he is involved in, people like him and are drawn to him in a remarkably short period of time. I think, after observing this phenomenon for the past several years, that it is at least in part due to the fact that he is unfailingly polite and equally open to everyone—except his sister, of course. Even when treated rudely, he continues to be polite to others, and they eventually respond in kind. I'm not sure how he learned to hone this gift (he certainly didn't catch it from me), but it works. Consequently, people want to spend time around him, are compelled to help him, and want to see him succeed. The gift of being polite and well mannered opens doors for him that might otherwise be closed, and it will probably help him to be successful throughout his lifetime, no matter what he chooses to accomplish.

> ## Manners for Young Gentlemen
>
> 1. Telephone etiquette—how to answer the telephone properly and take a message
> 2. Manners regarding women—helping seat her, holding doors open, walking on the outside of the sidewalk between a woman and traffic, standing when a woman enters a room
> 3. Personal manners—not dressing like a slob, not wearing a baseball cap or hat indoors, learning good personal hygiene
> 4. Table etiquette—not bolting his food, learning how to set a table, learning proper table manners, treating waitstaff properly in a restaurant

Courage

> Be on your guard; stand firm in the faith; be men of courage; be strong.
>
> 1 Corinthians 16:13

Edmund Burke said, "The only thing necessary for the triumph of evil is for good men to do nothing." It sure seems like a lot of men today are allowing evil to flourish just by doing nothing. One man who did do something to thwart evil was Todd Beamer.

On September 11, 2001, Todd Beamer, a Wheaton College graduate and evangelical Christian, was one of the passengers aboard United Airlines Flight 93 when it was hijacked by terrorists.

After passengers were herded to the back of the jet, Beamer called the GTE Customer Center in Oakbrook, Illinois. He told supervisor Lisa Jefferson about the hijacking. The passengers were planning to jump the terrorists, he said. And then he asked her to pray with him.

As Flight 93 hurtled toward destruction, Todd Beamer could not have known that his quiet prayers would ultimately be heard by millions—that the story of his last acts on earth would be a witness to the Lord he loved and serve as a lasting example of true heroism.

Up to this moment, Beamer had been all business. "Lisa," he said suddenly.

"Yes?" responded Jefferson.

"That's my wife's name," said Beamer.

"Well, that's my name too, Todd," said Jefferson.

"Oh, my God," said Beamer. "I don't think we're going to get out of this thing. I'm going to have to go out on faith."

Jefferson tried to comfort him. "Todd," she said, "you don't know that."

Beamer asked her to promise to call his wife if he didn't make it home. He told her about his little boys and the new baby on the way. Then he said that the passengers were going to try to jump the hijackers.

"Are you sure that's what you want to do, Todd?" asked Jefferson.

"It's what we have to do," he answered. He asked her to pray with him. Beamer kept a Lord's Prayer bookmark in his Tom Clancy novel, but he didn't need any prompting. He began to recite the litany, and she joined him: "Our Father, who art in heaven . . ."

After they finished, Beamer said, "Jesus, help me." He recited the Twenty-third Psalm. Then Jefferson heard him say:

"Are you guys ready? Let's roll."

We now know from the cockpit voice recorder that Beamer and other passengers wrestled with the hijackers and forced the plane to crash into the ground, killing themselves but foiling what was believed to have been the hijackers' plan to fly Flight 93 into the Capitol or the White House. It wasn't Todd Beamer's job to fight terrorists. He was just a passenger who along with several other brave men and women did what they didn't have to do and ended up foiling a terrible evil that might have been done to his country.

Todd Beamer was one of many heroes on Flight 93 that day. Whatever his heroism was inspired by, what matters most is that in the end, he *did* act heroically.[6]

Todd Beamer showed one kind of courage—physical courage. Other kinds of courage are just as difficult and just as heroic. Courage, or bravery, is simply doing what needs to be done even though you're scared and tired. It is the ability to confront fear in the face of pain, danger, uncertainty, or intimidation. It's not standing on the sidelines of complacency.

Teach your son to lead courageously, to stand by his convictions even when the consequences of those convictions may result in pain, sorrow, or unpleasant circumstances. Someday he will lead his own family. Fathers are faced with tough decisions every day. Sometimes it's easy to take the cowardly way out under pressure. The question is, do you want him to lead with courage or with cowardice?

Courage often requires the willingness to sacrifice for others. That's the kind of courage your son needs to lead a family—the courage to continue to do what is right even when all those around him are calling for him to compromise. The courage to sacrifice his needs and desires for the betterment of others. The courage to get up and go to work every day when he hates his job. The courage to stay married when he could more easily run off with the woman from work who "really understands me." The courage to live after a child has died. The courage to face, and possibly even overcome, a life-threatening disease. The courage to speak out against immorality when no one else seems to care. The courage to stand by his convictions in the face of overwhelming criticism.

Compassion

Our world has a great need for compassion, as this story illustrates:

> It's no secret that America is in the midst of a spiritual and moral crisis. Polls today indicate that most Americans are deeply concerned about the direction our nation is heading. The real problem is a critical shortage of people who care enough to get off the sidelines and make a difference. Sometimes it only takes one person to turn the flow from negative to positive.
>
> Take, for instance, Babe Ruth, the most famous baseball player of all time. The Babe finished his career in a slump, and according to one legendary story, he was jeered mercilessly one day in Cincinnati. As he made his customary trot off the field to the dugout, the fans began to yell obscenities at him. The booing intensified until a little boy jumped a fence

and ran to his hero's side. The child threw his arms around Babe's legs, crying as he fiercely hugged him. Moved by the young lad's display of affection and emotion, Ruth gently swept the boy upwards and into his arms. As they walked off the field, the man and boy cried together.

Suddenly, the hoots, howls and curses ceased. The eerie silence was replaced by a thunderous ovation. Fans of all ages now began to weep.[7]

Compassion is the ability to empathize with and have sympathy for another's feelings. It is the ability to extend mercy. If our sons do not learn this character trait, how will they ever be able to truly understand and appreciate God's gift to us? How too will they be able to competently father through situations in which they have no experience? Compassion will enable them to understand when their fifteen-year-old daughter's hormonal spikes cause her behavior to surge back and forth between calm rationality one minute and raging lunacy the next. Or to stay strong when everything in their world seems to be going wrong.

Self-Discipline and Self-Control

As we drove home from the county fair one afternoon, my son commented, "I hate it that you're so critical of other drivers. You always yell at them and criticize them."

My first thought was, *It's because they're all such knuckleheads.* My second thought was, *Oh, man, he's right.* I *was* being critical of every other driver on the road—every time I drove anywhere. For the past several years I had been ranting and raving whenever I went anywhere in the car. I was setting a horrible example for my wife and children, and they were sick of listening to me.

I was struck that not only was this a control issue that I needed to deal with, but it had also become a habit—one due to my own lack of self-discipline and self-control.

Self-discipline is doing what we don't want to do but should. Self-control is *not doing* something we want to do but shouldn't.

These two traits are different yet inexplicably interwoven. A lack of one or both of these character traits sinks more men and destroys more lives than any other character deficit. An absence of either of these traits leads men into addictions with drugs, gambling, pornography, drinking, and adultery—all of which are family-destroyers and soul-killers.

These character traits keep a man from doing things in private that he would never do in public. They are inner strengths that a man develops over time with exercise, like a muscle. Typically, if a man lacks self-discipline in one area of his life, he lacks self-control in other areas of his life as well.

Discipline, which is the core of self-discipline, is being able to control your life by having a sense of priorities, by putting first things first. Discipline governs thoughts and actions. In discipline, we have to work hard and develop right habits.[8]

How does a boy develop self-discipline and self-control? One of the ways to develop discipline is to keep score on ourselves. When a boy learns to monitor his own behavior against a code of ethics and principles established by his father, he develops self-discipline and eventually becomes responsible for his own life.

Another way he develops these traits is by being held responsible for his actions—our old friend accountability again. For instance, if your son's going to a movie is predicated upon his cleaning his room and he doesn't clean it . . . he can't go to the movie. If you told him no ice cream if he doesn't eat his dinner . . . then no ice cream if he doesn't eat his dinner—even if the rest of his siblings get ice cream. If he's disrespectful to you . . . well, let's just say he needs to learn early that it might be a little dangerous to disrespect dad. Let me qualify that last statement by saying that that's part of a father's influence—the fear factor. A father's job is to teach his son the fact that sometimes there are unpleasant consequences to unwise actions. I'm not promoting physical violence here, but unpleasant consequences usually only need to be endured one time to be effective in this type of situation. A big mistake some of today's "New Age" fathers make is allowing their kids to be disrespectful to them—I've seen it many times. Once the inherent, God-given respect with which you have been endowed is lost, you'll have a hard time getting it back.

You probably know some men whose names you would never associate with the words *self-discipline* or *self-control*. What do you think of those men? Probably not what you'd want people to think of when your son's name is mentioned. In this "instant gratification" world we live in, developing self-control and self-discipline may be the greatest gift you can give your son as he grows into manhood.

Honesty

You must pay for conformity. All goes well as long as you run with conformists. But you, who are honest men in other particulars, know, that there is alive somewhere a man whose honesty reaches to this point also, that he shall not kneel to false gods, and, on the day when you meet him, you sink into the class of counterfeits.

Ralph Waldo Emerson

The dictionary defines *honest* as "free from deception, truthful, genuine, real, reputable, credible, marked by integrity, frank, upright, just, conscientious, honorable." Are there any character traits listed here that you don't want your son to be known for?

One of the hardest things for a man to do is admit when he is wrong. While that's probably not earth-shattering news to any of us, be aware that your son struggles with the same natural inclination. Males are taught from a young age to always be right, to know how to fix things, to have all the answers. It's a heavy burden—one compounded by not being honest enough with ourselves and others to admit we are human. Men fall into a trap of believing they have to be perfect. It's a no-win situation, and we can start remedying the problem by learning how to admit when we are wrong and ask for forgiveness. Males have a much easier time being truthful with others if they are honest with themselves first.

In order to do this, a boy needs to learn about his own individual strengths and weaknesses. Some weaknesses, such as a lustful nature, are inherent in most men. By being honest with himself, a man can be aware of potential character pitfalls. For example, most people would consider me to be a diligent, hardworking man. And I am, but only because I know myself to be lazy in nature. I force myself (through self-discipline) to work hard because I know if I don't, my natural inclination toward laziness will surface and prevent me from fulfilling the destiny that God has planned for me. Likewise, men, because of their susceptibility to carnal lust, should stay away from areas of temptation such as pornography and strip clubs. Let your son know early on that you expect honesty from him at all times—then model that behavior yourself. A man who is honest with himself is honest to others.

A man's word is his bond. In fact, a man's word is the measure of his character. If you give your word to someone, you are making a covenant with that person. So if you tell your wife, son, or daughter that you love them, then turn around and verbally abuse them, break your promises, or act irresponsibly, you have not lived up to your word. You cannot love someone and simultaneously lie to them. It is incongruous behavior. Honesty keeps us from making those kinds of mistakes in our lives.

One NFL pre-game show asks players being interviewed whether they would rather be known as "nice" or "honest." I'm always surprised at how many men respond "nice." Little white lies to protect someone's feelings are not necessarily innocent. The art of diplomacy, good manners, and honesty will serve your son better throughout life than even a small lie.

Humility

Integrity begins with humility. Most young men are filled with pride—I was. But pride infects our thought process and keeps us from being all that we are capable of being. Remember, it's not about us.

The opposite of pride is humility. Humility is what allows men to achieve great things for a purpose higher than themselves. This includes putting their family's well-being ahead of their own wants and desires. Peter says this about humility: "All of you, clothe yourselves with humility toward one another, because, 'God opposes the proud but gives grace to the humble'" (1 Peter 5:5).

But humility seems to have gotten a bad rap today. If someone, especially a man, is called humble or exhibits humility, the connotation is that he is a wimp. Humility is somehow associated with being humiliated, while pride is looked upon as a virtue. Young men are supposed to be confident, cocky, overachieving go-getters who never admit they're wrong.

However, the Webster's dictionary defines *humble* as (1) not proud or haughty, (2) not pretentious; unassuming, (3) modest. All in all, pretty good character traits. Some of the wisest, happiest, and most successful men I know are extremely humble individuals.

The Bible says this about pride: "Pride goes before destruction, a haughty spirit before a fall" (Prov. 16:18). And about pride versus humility it says: "A man's pride will bring him low, but the humble in spirit will retain honor" (Prov. 29:23 NKJV).

The older I get, the more stock I put in humility. Maybe it's because humility comes with maturity.

Men who are humble are often *gentle* as well—another word that has gotten a bad image in our culture. Understand that meekness or gentleness is not necessarily weakness. Gentleness is really power under control. Jesus was gentle, but no man ever walked the earth with more power—Jesus just controlled his power. I've heard gentleness likened to the quivering muscles of a mighty warhorse awaiting battle— power under control. Men who are confident of their place in the world are like powerful, humble warhorses.

We need to teach our sons humility—the humility that comes from others having faith in us.

Trustworthiness

Because of my background, I grew up believing that those closest to me continually let me down. I vowed at an early age, even before consciously realizing it, that I would never rely on or trust anyone. I believed that I was the only one I could depend on. Since then I've learned that you have to depend not only on God but on other people as well. As men, we must have other people in our lives in order to function properly.

To trust someone is to know that he will stand beside you—that he won't cut and run when the going gets tough. Preston Gillham says, "Trust is the confidence that continues to believe, even if what you believe appears to be untrue. To my way of thinking, trust is one step deeper than faith."[9]

One of the ways I typically evaluate a man's character is asking whether I would trust him to cover my back in battle. Some people (usually men I wouldn't trust in battle) have commented that it's a harsh way to judge someone, but I don't think it is. We are in a war—a spiritual war—and we need people around us we can trust to cover our backs—people who put our well-being ahead of their own. We need men who care enough about us and have our best interests at heart so much that they are willing to challenge our actions and decisions even if we get angry with them.

Men who are trustworthy are dependable. Can he be counted upon? Is his word his bond? Are his wife, children, and friends confident that he will be there for them when times are tough? A man who is dependable can be counted on to do what is best for you and others around him.

These are the kind of men we need as leaders. The Bible puts it this way: "But select capable men from all the people, men who fear God, trustworthy men who hate dishonest gain; and appoint them as officials over thousands, hundreds, fifties and tens. Have them serve as judges for the people at all times; let them bring every difficult case to you, but the simple ones they can decide themselves" (Exod. 18:21–22).

Talk to your son about your own life and what being able to trust someone means to you. If you have trouble trusting due to past experiences, discuss it with him so that he can understand how trustworthiness is such a strong character trait in a man and how damaging it can be when violated.

Honor: The Essence of a Noble Man

A man realizes that he is in a unique position to give honor like no one else, and that no one can truly replace that responsibility for him. He avoids sarcasm, put-downs, belittling words, and ways that diminish the honor of a person.

Stu Weber, *Four Pillars of a Man's Heart*

Our discussion of the positive character traits that make a noble man can be summed up in one sentence: A noble man is a man of honor.

Hold your son to the higher standard of honor. Honor defines the character of a man. Character is like granite, withstanding the winds and rains of our culture.

In the movie *Rob Roy*, Liam Neeson plays Robert Roy MacGregor, a clan chieftain in the early 1700s Scottish Highlands. At the beginning of the movie, Rob Roy has the following conversation with his two young sons about honor:

Son: Father, will MacGregors ever be kings again?
RR: All men with honor are kings. But not all kings have honor.
Son: What is honor?
RR: Honor is . . . what no man can give you, and none can take away. Honor is a man's gift to himself.
Son: Do women have it?
RR: Women are the heart of honor, and we cherish and protect it in them. You must never mistreat a woman or malign a man, or stand by and see another do so.
Son: How do you know if you have it?
RR: Never worry on the getting of it. It grows in you and speaks to you. All you need do is listen.

Fathers have been positioned by God to have a powerful influence to bestow honor on their families. When you teach your son the dignity of honor, you give him a noble vision of masculinity.

In the movie *The Last Samurai*, Tom Cruise plays Captain Woodrow Algrin, a highly decorated Civil War hero. Algrin is compelled to drink himself into a stupor every day in order to live with the atrocities he's witnessed and committed during battle. Hired by the Japanese government to teach modern warfare to the new Japanese feudal army, he is captured in the first battle by the last remaining band of samurai.

The samurai were Japan's warrior class for seven centuries. They served as private soldiers, protecting their *daimyio* or "lord." The word *samurai* literally means "those who serve." As hereditary warriors they were governed by a strict code of ethics—*bushido*, meaning "the way of the warrior"—that defined service and conduct appropriate to their status as elite members of Japanese society. Their code required a lot of physical hardship, absolute devotion to duty, and bravery in all things. It also revolved around a complex system of honor and respect.

After living with the samurai for the winter, Cruise's character, Algrin, is captivated by their lifestyle and code of conduct. Algrin eventually regains his honor by fighting for the samurai's noble cause. One scene sums up his belief in the importance of the honor code of the samurai. The leader of the samurai, believing defeat is imminent, is contemplating committing suicide in order to avoid the shame of defeat.

Algrin says, "Shame? Shame for a life of service, discipline, compassion?"

"The way of the samurai is not necessary anymore."

"Necessary? What could be more necessary?"

The French call it *noblesse oblige*—the obligation of honorable, generous, and responsible behavior associated with high rank or birth. Honor seems to be one of the key ingredients in fulfilling a man's life, no matter his nationality or race.

And yet our culture does not promote honor within men. C. S. Lewis said, "We laugh at honor and are shocked to find traitors in our midst. We castrate, and bid the geldings be fruitful."[10] Our world does not seem to hold honor in very high regard; at least, we seldom tout it when it is observed. Then we expect men to act honorably and are shocked when they don't.

Men need honor. It is essential to our being. Michael Gurian says,

> Honor and honor codes are essential to boys and men. Because males are both hardwired and soft wired for performance, they are very conscious of how they perform. Boys develop personal codes of honor, and they are sponge-like in their absorption of codes of honor suggested to them by their nurturing systems. They watch their parents' honor codes like hawks, remembering every detail. They are vulnerable to the honor codes provided them by mentors. If parents, mentors, and educators don't provide them with honor training, they will learn honor codes from peers, who sometimes promote codes that are dangerous.[11]

Being honorable and having the ability to give honor are important factors in becoming an effective husband and father. Honor often requires us to put others' needs ahead of our own. Gurian continues,

> If I do not have a well-developed sense of honor, I will become undisciplined and probably somewhat dangerous in my relationships when they confuse me. Without a clear sense of honor, I have little firm ground to stand on, and I often become overwhelmed by the wants of another person. . . . Adult males and females who have been trained in compassion and sensitivity but not honor end up destroying their marriages. They do not have the inner strength to pull back into the self and hold on while the

partner goes through immense, confusing inner changes of his or her own.[12]

I used to look at honoring others from the wrong perspective. I used to think some people weren't worthy of being given honor.

Gary Smalley did too. He says,

I used to think you had to like people to honor them. I thought they had to be performing well before you could honor them. But honor has nothing to do with performance. It has everything to do with attitude. Honor is a gift of grace. It shows the other person that you value him or her. Honor is something you give a person without his having to earn it. Did we earn the love of God? No. Did Christ come to die in your place because you did something worthwhile? No. While we were yet sinners, Christ died for us. We were shaking our fists in God's face, saying we didn't want Him, yet He sent His son to die for us because He valued us so dearly.[14]

> **Teaching Honor**
>
> How do you teach honor to your son? In order to focus your energies on this question, take a moment to answer these questions:
>
> - Have I modeled loyalty this week? Have I talked with my boy about the loyalty I was modeling?
> - Have I modeled duty this week? Have I talked with my boy about my duties and his?
> - Have I modeled fairness this week? Have I talked with my boy about why I made those decisions about fairness?[13]

I want my son to have honor. To stand tall as the fierce winds of adversity blow around him. To cherish and protect women and children. To fight for justice and equality. To stand for *something*.

How about you? What character traits do you want people to think of when your son's name is mentioned?

In this chapter we discussed some of the qualities a boy needs to develop in order to reach his potential as a man. This was not an exhaustive list. Nor can you reasonably expect your son to master all of the traits summarized here. However, by being aware of what character traits you admire and respect in a man, you can more easily help your son develop a powerful vision of masculinity as he grows older.

Your son needs to understand that no man is an island. His choices and the decisions he makes affect other people's lives whether he is willing to admit it or not. Our decisions impact other lives like a pebble dropping in a pond creates ripples across the surface. When your son becomes a father, his decisions will create ripples in people's lives for generations thereafter. Teach your son that his family name stands for honor. Honor will create a legacy in your lineage that will change the world.

Questions for Reflection and Discussion

1. Make a list of character traits you want your son to have. Discuss with other men why these traits are important in general and to you in particular. How can you help instill these traits in your son?
2. Think of the best example you've witnessed of manly behavior and discuss it with your son.
3. Tell your son what you think makes a man. Ask him what character traits he thinks are manly.

7

Discipline

Discipline isn't just punishing, forcing compliance or stamping out bad behavior. Rather, discipline has to do with teaching proper deportment, caring about others, controlling oneself and putting some-one else's wishes before one's own when the occasion calls for it.

Lawrence Balter, *Who's in Control?*

WE SHARE OUR home with a dog named Riley. Riley is a dun-colored, 110-pound cur with the disposition of a teddy bear. Part German shepherd and part Labrador retriever, Riley's an all-American mutt that thinks my son is his litter mate. Riley is four years old now, but he still looks and acts like a clumsy, barrel-chested mongrel puppy. He has oversized ears (which prick straight up to their fullest glory whenever the words *walk*, *car*, or *biscuit* are murmured) and a long, bulbous snout attached to a hard, lumpy skull. As near as I can tell, he sleeps on one or the other of the kids' beds all day long until they get home from school. Then he plays until it's time to go back to bed. Quite a stressful life he leads. Riley's bark is hoarse and cracks like he's perpetually in puberty, and he still hasn't figured out how to lift his leg like every other male dog I've ever seen. I think he's afraid of everything and everybody, but he puts up a good front—good, that is, until he rolls over on his back exposing his belly in submission at the drop of a hat.

Frankly, Riley's not the smartest creature God ever created, but he *is* extremely intelligent in matters pertaining to his own self-gratification. Riley loves dog biscuits, and my wife has made it her mission to teach him to do tricks. For each successful trick, Riley is rewarded with a piece of dog biscuit. Much to my surprise, Riley has learned over the years how to crawl, roll over, sit, shake, stand, and lie down. He has even learned to stay away from a biscuit (or other food) that has been set down on the floor in front of him. He has developed the self-control to keep away from the biscuit on command even when Suzanne leaves the room for an extended period of time. When she reenters the room, she will find him still sitting and staring intently at the biscuit. But he will not make any attempt to snatch the treat in her absence. My wife has taught Riley the trait of self-discipline by imposing a series of consequences and rewards to produce a desired behavior.

Self-Discipline

All children need clear-cut rules, structure, and guidelines. They thrive under firm supervision and guidance. But boys, even more than girls, need strong boundaries and discipline from the adults, especially older males, in their lives.

134

Discipline comes in two forms—internal and external. Internal discipline, or self-discipline, is what we strive to teach our sons by applying external discipline. External discipline is applied in a variety of forms: allowing them to suffer the consequences of their actions, teaching them the pleasures of delayed gratification, showing them the relationship between hard work and success, and teaching them personal accountability. Boys who are not subjected to healthy discipline while growing up tend to live unhappy lives and create chaos in the lives of those around them. When we discipline our sons, we are actually preparing them for much more fulfilling lives.

The Bible says that accepting chastening, or developing self-discipline, is a good thing. Hebrews 12:7 says, "If you endure chastening, God deals with you as with sons; for what son is there whom a father does not chasten?" (NKJV). In other words, sons are naturally disciplined by their fathers out of love.

The book of Proverbs talks often about a father's duty to teach his child discipline. "He who spares his rod hates his son, but he who loves him disciplines him promptly" (Prov. 13:24 NKJV). This is followed closely by Proverbs 15:10, which says, "Harsh discipline is for him who forsakes the way, and he who hates correction will die" (NKJV). And lest we forget, "The rod and rebuke give wisdom, but a child left to himself brings shame to his mother" (Prov. 29:15 NKJV).

God the Father even gets into the act: "My son, do not despise the chastening of the LORD, nor detest His correction; For whom the LORD loves He corrects, just as a father the son in whom he delights" (Prov. 3:11–12 NKJV).

We learned about self-discipline as a character trait of noble masculinity earlier in this book. But we need to delve more deeply into this most essential character trait for men.

Here are some reasons why teaching your son discipline is imperative to his growth as a man.

Consequences and Accountability

Boys need structure and supervision. They need to be "civilized." Males must be accountable to someone other than themselves, such as their wife, other men, their father, and God. God has designed us so that we need other people—people who will help hold us accountable to God's laws. Without that accountability, we tend to make our own rules and codes of conduct. Boys from an early age need to learn that their actions have positive or negative consequences. And they need to learn that their decisions affect not just them but others as well. A man's ability to let other people into his life is an important part of willingness to maintain accountability. This kind of openness is a skill in which boys need to be trained. Accountability helps keep males from falling into temptation with soul-killers such as drugs, alcohol abuse, gambling, pornography, and adultery. These kinds of temptation, which we know destroy families, are one reason why men and boys need accountability in their lives. Training your son to resist temptation and fill his life with righteousness will also build character in him.

Young people also need to be accountable to someone who will push them to exert the effort required in order to achieve their best. A father can apply some of this pressure, but he often needs to bring in outside influences as well. For this reason, involving your son in an organized sport or other activity such as music, art, or other trades can provide him with both a character-building training ground and an accountability partner in the person of the coach or teacher. A coach's (or teacher's) job description has traditionally been to get more effort and talent out of his players or students than they are capable of extracting from themselves. In addition, a coach's goal is also to teach boys character traits such as hard work, respect, self-discipline, and teamwork.

Unfortunately, our culture, with its emphasis on self-esteem and equality, sometimes encourages parents to sabotage the accountability process. For example, in an effort to teach a young man respect and self-discipline, a high school coach can do one of several things. He can take away a player's starting position, limit his playing time, reprimand him in private, or verbally challenge him in front of the team to improve his performance and practice habits. A young man who has never been subjected to accountability in his life often reacts negatively when disciplined this way. Upon being subjected to what he perceives as unfair treatment, the young man runs home crying about how the coach abused him. His parents, of course, are aghast and immediately charge down to complain to the school superintendent. This all too often results in the coach getting fired (sometimes without even being allowed to tell his side of the story), followed by the coach appealing to the local school board for justice. The board, more often concerned with funding and public relations than with finding the truth, usually backs the superintendent's decision.

During a recent meeting on the firing of a local high school boys' baseball coach for allegedly mistreating his players, the one dissenting school board member stated, "I think we are confusing teaching discipline and respect with something else." Ironically, the board voted unanimously that the coach did not verbally or physically abuse anyone on the team but still upheld the superintendent's firing of him.

By running too quickly to rescue our sons when things get tough, we teach them that the way out of hard times is to find someone to get them off the hook rather than teaching them to be accountable to the one in authority. This establishes patterns that will influence them throughout their lives. A boy who avoids accountability becomes a man who is answerable to no one—a recipe for disaster. A situation like the coaching situation just described is a good opportunity to let him learn that he must be accountable for the consequences of his actions. And your role as a father is also to teach your son to submit to legitimate authorities in his life, male or female. You best do this by supporting their authority and decisions.

By rescuing your son, you may also be training him to base his decision-making skills on feelings instead of principles. Emotions are unreliable and subject to change on a whim. Principles are like lighthouses that guide ships away from treacherous rocks that would tear holes in their hulls, sinking the ship and killing all aboard.

As a coach, I may know more about your child than you do in some areas of his or her life. I see young men and women under competitive and stressful situations. I work with them intensely for hours every day. I know how they react when challenged and how best to motivate them under certain circumstances. I know what their strengths and weaknesses are. I usually discover what kind of character they have very quickly. And sometimes I even know about personal dilemmas they struggle with that their parents aren't aware of. However, I have never had a parent come up to me and ask me about his or her child. I suspect teachers develop the same knowledge of their students as well. It's unfortunate that parents and coaches or teachers don't work together more often for the best interests of the child.

Coaches are not the only authority figures who should hold boys accountable for their behavior. It's equally important for other males—even those who are peripherally involved—to hold boys accountable for their actions. My son and I try to go on wilderness camping trips each summer.

We pack up whatever we can carry on our backs and hike into a remote area of wilderness for four to five days, living off the land and whatever fish we can catch. We carry some freeze-dried food just in case we need it. Several years ago we went to the Strawberry Mountain Wilderness in eastern Oregon. On the way home we took a detour and stopped at the tiny town of Fossil, Oregon, to dig up some fossils on the side of the hill above the high school football field. Later we stopped at the only ice cream parlor/casket shop west of the Mississippi. As we sat drinking a delicious milkshake, an interesting event took place.

Several tables over from ours sat two local teenage girls, a baby, and a scruffy-looking young man who was evidently dating one of the girls. After several minutes a giant of a man walked in with his two little girls. It was clear that the big man knew the teenage girls, as they introduced him to the young man accompanying them. As if suspecting what was to come, the young ladies scurried off to the ice cream counter with the baby and the man's little girls. The big man reached out and said hello, engulfing the younger man's hand in his giant paw. Much to the younger male's surprise, he didn't let go of his hand as their discussion continued. I smiled as I overheard the conversation. While I couldn't hear the younger man's responses, he became more and more visibly uncomfortable as the following discussion ensued:

Big Guy:	What's your name, son?
Young Fellow:	Mumble, mumble.
Big Guy:	What school do you go to? Where do you live?
Young Fellow:	Mutter, mumble—mutter.
Big Guy:	What's your daddy's name?
Young Fellow:	Mumble, squeak.
Big Guy:	Your family the Smith people over near the town of John Day?

Young Fellow: Hsmnt.

Big Guy: I know your daddy—he's a good man. Son, nice meetin' ya. Y'all have fun, and treat these girls right now.

He let go of the boy's hand and walked off to the ice cream counter as the young man nearly crumpled in relief. The big guy had effectively said, "I know who you are, I know where to find you, and I know your family. If anything happens to these girls, you'll be accountable to me." That's how men hold younger males accountable for their actions. I guarantee you, that young man will think twice before doing something irresponsible with or to those young ladies. That big man had no vested interest in protecting those girls except the responsibility every man has to look after and protect women. Also, I suspect that gentleman hopes that other men will look after his daughters in the same way when they get older. Unfortunately, this type of manly accountability probably only happens in small rural communities anymore—if at all.

Challenging Authority

Boys have a natural tendency to challenge authority. It's part of developing the leadership skills that they will need later in life as men. However, a boy needs to learn when leading is appropriate and when following is appropriate. Dads play an intrinsic role in that process. Fathers, blessed with the innate "fear factor" that God has instilled in their children, are well suited to teach boys when challenging authority is appropriate and when it's not. Sometimes the consequences of mistakes in that area can be quite unpleasant. Better your son learn that lesson in a safe environment with you than later when it could have more serious consequences.

For example, as Frank entered adolescence, hormones that he hadn't yet learned to control kicked in. One day he naturally got a little "mouthy" with his mother. Luckily, I happened to overhear his disrespect. I immediately got in his face, saying, "That's my wife you're talking to. I wouldn't let another man talk to her that way, and I'm sure not going to allow you to do it." Needless to say, that one time seems to have done the trick. Not that he hasn't gotten lippy now and then, but when he starts to and sees me look at him, he seems to remember our conversation and makes the effort to control his mouth. Again, this is an example of his using self-discipline to avoid unpleasant consequences.

As your son develops his leadership skills, you're apt to bump heads every now and then. My son is eighteen years old now. He's developing his critical thinking skills, so he likes to argue. It seems like no matter what I say, he will disagree just to argue with me. He's also going through his know-it-all stage. He certainly knows how to push my buttons. Our home sometimes seems like a young bull and an old bull butting heads in the same pasture. I think it's God's way of preparing him to leave home and preparing (motivating) me to let him go. Otherwise he might be inclined to stay forever.

We can't expect our sons to be blindly submissive to every authority figure they encounter—nor would we want them to be. But the proper way to disagree or even challenge authority is not by being disrespectful. Teach your son to think through the reasons he disagrees with someone in authority, not just to react emotionally, and then to present his opinions respectfully, in a logical manner, with reasonable evidence to support his conclusions. This will allow him to disagree while not making the other person feel threatened. It will also garner him respect and help him develop his leadership skills.

Coincidently, while I was writing this section, my daughter, Kelsey, came down and snuck a letter addressed to me onto my desk. Kelsey has always been what we politely refer to in mixed company as a "strong-willed" child. She has many good character traits that will someday serve her well in life. Our challenge has been to teach her to control some of her less positive personality traits in order not to sabotage herself until she matures enough to use her strengths wisely. Her letter to me was a very well thought out and respectfully presented opinion on why she should be able to do something that I would normally not agree with. In this case, the forethought she used tells me she has thought through most of the issues and is responsible enough for me to trust her judgment in this situation. So I changed my mind and allowed her the freedom to make her own decision.

Meeting life's various challenges helps prepare your son for the time when he's the authority in his own life. Help your son understand the natural process God is putting him through, one of balancing self-respect with respect for others. It will benefit him and protect your future relationship.

Anger Control

Too many of us men use anger as a weapon to attack others or as a shield to protect our feelings. Then we pass that coping mechanism on to our sons as a way to deal with and express their frustrations.

Anger is a God-given emotion. It is the second most often mentioned emotion in the Bible—second only to love. However, anger in men is a secondary emotion often used to mask other emotions. Gary and Carrie Oliver say this about anger in males:

Anger is often the only emotion that a male is aware of, though they've surely experienced a myriad of other emotions as well. For just below the surface, a man has many other, deeper emotions that need to be identified and acknowledged. Hidden underneath (sometimes deep underneath) the surface emotion of anger is fear, hurt, frustration, disappointment, vulnerability, and longing for connection. Boys learn early on that anger can help them deflect attention from these more painful emotions. Anger is safer, and it provides some protection for the frightened and vulnerable self. Anger helps him avoid, or at least minimize, his pain. Anger provides a surge of energy. It decreases his vulnerability and increases his sense of security. What's more, he tells himself, all real men get angry. In short, boys learn quickly that it's easier to feel anger than it is to feel pain.[1]

Having been raised in an alcoholic home, I was brought up in a culture steeped in fear—fear of everything from whether the ambulance would come to our house that night to the unpredictable reaction that even the most innocent facial expression might provoke. A loud noise was guaranteed to arouse an angry reaction in a parent with a hangover. I felt like the ground was never steady under my feet and the rug might get jerked out from under me at any moment. Because of that, sudden loud noises provoke a fearful reaction in me to this day. That fear response manifests itself in anger as a self-defense mode. Of course my kids know about this response, and they actually get a charge out of inciting that reaction from me by startling me with loud noises. It's sort of like poking a sleeping bear with a stick, I guess.

As a very young man I realized that anger conquered my fear. If I just got mad, I never had to face the humiliating emotion of being afraid again. After I reached a certain size, my anger protected me, my brothers and sisters, and even my mother from physical abuse. I remember saying to myself, "Never again will I be afraid of anything or anybody." Of course, that was ridiculous. I spent the majority of my adult life being afraid of many things; however, I covered it by being angry. Unfortunately, fear and anger are lonely companions. But I clearly remember the moment when I understood the power of anger and how it kept me from acknowledging my fear.

Jim used anger to control his fear too. Jim's dad was an abusive alcoholic who beat Jim and his mother. According to Jim, his dad was so angry during his bouts of drunkenness that many times he would come home and "paint the kitchen with my blood." Jim grew up angry and discovered football as an outlet for his anger. He played with a ferocity that earned him All-American honors in high school. He was recruited to play in college, where he continued to vent his anger on the football field. He was eventually drafted into the National Football League.

Jim says that in college, during his frequent trips to the bars at night, anytime he would see a man look at a woman the wrong way, he would beat the stuffing out of him. He fought many times, always in anger. Just like his dad. Jim never lost a fight.

But during his junior year at college, he ran smack dab into an opponent he couldn't beat—the cross. A man from Campus Crusade for Christ shared the gospel with him. Jim looked up to God and called him "Father" that night. Immediately the fighting ended.

Several years later, Jim started hanging out with a famous Christian author. This man encouraged Jim to reconcile with his father—to ask his father for forgiveness. Jim said, "I'll never go to my father and ask for forgiveness. I'm not responsible for what happened when I was a child."

His friend persisted, "Are you sure that you bear no responsibility whatsoever for your relationship with your father today?"

"Well, maybe 3 percent of our problems are my fault, but 97 percent is his fault!" he cried.

"Well, Jim, as a Christian it is your responsibility to accept 100 percent of the blame for your 3 percent of fault."

So Jim went home and met with his father. "Dad, will you please forgive me for putting you on a pedestal that you couldn't live up to? Please forgive me for comparing you to my coaches and my girlfriends' fathers."

His dad said, "No! I will never forgive you, because if I did, *I* would be stuck holding the bag!"

Left with no other choice, Jim lifted his hands to God, right there in front of his dad, and cried out, "Father, please, if there is any way to touch my father's heart and soften his pain, please, God, help him."

Jim's father broke down in tears and said, "I've never heard anyone talk to God that way." Reaching his hands to the sky, he sobbed, "Please, God, if you could ever love me, please come into my heart too."

Jim and his dad spent the next fourteen good years as father and son.[2]

Help your son learn to understand the underlying causes of anger and then to control this potentially destructive emotion. An understanding of the emotions behind anger can often act as a signpost to point toward healing, as it did with Jim. Far beyond just controlling and identifying our emotions, understanding the cause of our reactions can lead to healing within ourselves and healing in our relationships.

Teach Him to Work

Sixteen years ago, I was working as the plant superintendent for a large food processing company. During the fruit harvest season of spring, summer, and fall, I was required to work sixteen-hour days, seven days a week. I hated the job and the working conditions. I had accepted the job because it paid well and had good insurance benefits. With a growing family and a newly born child suffering from a birth anomaly that required multiple surgeries, I had no choice but to live up to my responsibilities and keep working. For six to seven months out of the year, I rarely, if ever, saw my family. Between work and travel time, I was home long enough only to shower and sleep for a few hours each day. Suzanne claimed she could see me dying before her eyes, and I felt like a walking zombie most of the time.

I remember driving over the I-205 bridge twice a day, to and from work. The sun was usually just rising or just setting as I crossed the three-mile bridge spanning the mighty Columbia River between Oregon and Washington. Every day as I crossed the bridge, I looked down and saw dozens of sailboats sailing down the river. My constant thought was, *What on earth do those people do that gives them the income and freedom to live that lifestyle?* Those images eventually motivated me to start my own business as a way to attempt to gain some control over my own destiny.

Many years later, I had forgotten all about those desperate days driving across the bridge. One day I found myself under the midmorning sun traveling across the same bridge on my way to an afternoon Seattle Mariner's baseball game. As is sometimes the case (although not as often anymore), I was bemoaning my life and all the struggles God was allowing me to wallow in. As I looked down and saw the sailboats on the water's surface, I remembered that longing I used to experience as I drove over the bridge. Then the thought suddenly struck me, *Hey, here I am in the middle of a workday with the time and resources to go to a professional baseball game. I am able to come and go pretty much as I choose. I'm one of those people I used to envy so much! Thank you so much, God, for blessing my life.*

I achieved that freedom only because I was willing to work harder than others. From a young age I was blessed with a good work ethic—one of the positive traits my parents instilled in me. I was willing to do the little things that add up to success. Nearly everyone does the big things to get ahead. But those who are willing to take on all the small, unpleasant details that no one else wants to do are the ones who gradually succeed.

Boys need to learn to work. One of the basic tenets of manhood is the need to work. We have to work; it's part of our makeup. Give boys chores at an early age. It keeps them busy and teaches them responsibility. Teach them to budget money by giving them a small allowance.

Let your son help you with your chores around the house. Patiently teach him *how* to do certain tasks. Sometimes I find myself asking my son to do something I think is simple, only to realize that no one (namely me) has ever shown him how.

I started earning money with lawn-mowing jobs and a newspaper route at age twelve. One mistake I'm convinced I made is not making my children begin working at an earlier age. And while they did have chores throughout childhood, we never adequately enforced the consequences of not completing them. Now, as I am getting ready to launch my kids out into the world, I'm concerned that I have not taught them the work ethic required in order to succeed in our world.

One of the major factors in marital failure in our country is financial pressure, and my son will one day face such pressure to support and provide for his own family. Fathers face tough decisions in these areas all the time. I recently read about a father who, rather than have his children attend a hopelessly inadequate public school in a crime-infested neighborhood, moved his family into an attic so he could afford to send his kids to a private Catholic school. A tough choice, but I admire him for it!

I also wish I had spent more time teaching my son how to budget his money. Because my wife and I didn't learn certain skills early in life—such as how to properly budget our resources and consistently save a portion of our monthly income—we have found ourselves hampered with constant debt management and sometimes poor stewardship of the resources with which God has blessed us. These things have probably decreased our effectiveness in doing God's work and God's willingness to utilize us.

Preparation for work and financial responsibility is one of the biggest factors that determines a person's success or failure. "Luck" is just being well prepared and ready to act when opportunity knocks. Does your son know how to look at a project you've given him and break it down into its separate components? Can he then design a plan to accomplish each phase of the project in the proper order? Can he balance a checkbook? Does he know to tithe 10 percent to God right off the top of his income and then save 10 percent after that? Does he know how devastating improperly used credit can be and how hard it is to pay off credit card debt?

These are all skills he will need to be proficient in when he goes out into the world. His wife and children will depend on his financial acumen. Preparing him well in these areas will give him a big advantage and head start in life.

Questions for Reflection and Discussion

1. In what areas of your son's life are you holding him accountable? Have you given another man permission to hold you accountable?

2. Look for times your son gets angry. Discuss with him the possible underlying reasons he reacted in anger. Was he really scared, frustrated, intimidated, hungry, or something else?
3. What chores have you assigned your son? How is he held accountable to complete them?
4. If your son is still young, decide *before* he gets to the appropriate age how you will develop a work ethic in him.

8

Loving Your Wife

*There is probably no greater satanic stronghold in
our culture than the idea of disposable marriage, . . .
it's eating away at the very heart of our nation. . . .
Marriage is the centerpiece of civilization.*

Stu Weber, *Spirit Warrior*

PERHAPS THE GREATEST gift you can give your son is to teach
him how to love his wife. Males aren't born knowing
how to love a woman, and boys need to be taught by example.
Should your son grow up to marry and have a family, he will
need your positive example as a husband more than probably
anything else you can teach him.

Abraham Lincoln is credited with having said, "The greatest gift a man can give his children is to love their mother."
Your son is watching how you treat your wife to see how
he should treat the women in his life. Your daughter is also

watching to see how she should expect to be treated by her future boyfriends and husband.

Ken Canfield says,

> All children are born as bachelors and bachelorettes. The first impression they have of marriage is what they observe in their own parents' union. They're watching you. They're taking notes. Your sons, however subconsciously, are asking the question: What does it mean to be a husband? They are also trying to figure out who these creatures called women are, and they are looking to you to see how you perceive them and what respect you give to them. Your daughters also have their eye on you. To submit to another in the mystery of marriage can be a fearful thing; your daughters are asking themselves how well their mother fared in the deal.[1]

Your wife is God's gift to you and should be valued and loved as much as you love yourself. You are the steward of your wife's love. Peter says, "Husbands, in the same way be considerate as you live with your wives, and treat them with respect as the weaker partner and as heirs with you of the gracious gift of life, so that nothing will hinder your prayers" (1 Peter 3:7). That's a foreign concept to most of us, and your son needs to be exposed to this type of mentality before he decides to become a husband.

Meeting Her Needs

As I am writing this chapter, I am listening to my wife sing while she is puttering around in the kitchen upstairs. Over the years I've noticed that whenever she is most fulfilled, she sings or hums to herself. I can't think of any greater feeling than hearing her singing and knowing she is feeling content with her life.

Your wife has a God-given desire to have a close relationship with you. It's one of her greatest needs in life.

> Dr. Willard F. Harley Jr. interviewed over twenty-two hundred women and listed their top five needs. The fifth greatest need of a woman was family commitment. Number four was financial support. Number three was honesty and openness with her husband. Number two was conversation. The greatest need of a woman—and this may surprise you—was affection. Women want nonsexual affection: tender words, letters, a gentle touch, affection that is given without any demand to meet our needs as men. A servant leader asks God to help him learn to fulfill his wife's needs.[2]

To be a servant leader for your wife, you must first be aware of her needs. Even if you think you already understand your wife, I challenge you to ask her to list her five greatest needs. I think you'll be surprised at what you find out. Suzanne and I go on a weekend retreat every few years. This gives me an opportunity to ask her about her needs and how I can help meet them. You'll discover that your wife's needs will change as she goes through different stages of life. When our kids were younger, Suzanne needed me to be more involved in day-to-day activities—to give her a mental and physical break from constant child care. Now, with our children nearly grown, one of the things she needs from me is support and encouragement as she attempts to achieve new personal goals.

Ask your wife where she'd like to be in life five or ten years from now. Then find ways you can help her achieve her dreams and goals. You may need to help her with this. Women are often more focused on the here and now, spending their energies on meeting others' needs instead of thinking of their own long-term plans. For instance, would your wife like to go back to school to get an advanced degree after the kids are grown? How about taking up painting or learning to play the piano? Maybe she'd like to enter the workforce and develop a career. Help her find what will satisfy her throughout the different stages of life, and then help her achieve those goals.

Besides the needs Harley discovered in his survey, your wife also has a significant need for security. You can meet that need best by making sure she understands that she is the most important person in your life and that you love and honor her. As you accomplish this, you might also end up fulfilling her need for affection as well. If your wife is uptight or nervous, perhaps her requirement for security is not being met. Usually once that need is met, most women are more relaxed.

So how can you help your wife feel your love and honor? You can start by mentioning it once in a while. Saying "I love you" is always a good place to start. We've all heard the old story about the man who said, "I told my wife I loved her when we got married. If anything changes, I'll let her know." Remember, just as much as you need respect, she needs to feel loved. She needs you to tell her you love her because she's more attuned to auditory cues in the same way that you're more visually wired.

Sometimes our actions speak louder than our words. Show her that you think about her by doing unexpected things every now and then. Bring her flowers for no reason. You don't have to be in the doghouse to buy flowers, you know. I try to remember to bring my wife "just 'cuz" flowers every so often. I give them to her "just 'cuz" I love her. Send her flowers at work so her coworkers can coo over them. Your wife feels special when her female counterparts are envious of how her husband treats her. I've found over the years that an inexpensive little trinket, like a silly flower or a card, means more to her than anything. I know this might not make sense to you or me, but I promise you that the rewards of letting her know you are thinking of her are well worth the effort. I try to spoil my wife whenever possible. She deserves it. She certainly put up with enough nonsense from me during our early years of marriage when I was trying to get my act together. She stuck with me through thick and thin, even when I was not deserving of her love and loyalty. Now she deserves to reap the benefits of her faithfulness.

The way you treat your wife throughout the day, especially when you give her respect, shows her she is special in your eyes. Thank her frequently (in front of the kids, of course) for that delicious meal she just cooked. Offer to go shopping with her without her asking you. (I know, I know, but it's important to her.) When you go shopping with your wife, slow down and let her set the pace. If you're like me, you shop by hunting down what you want and shooting it as efficiently and quickly as possible. But your wife probably likes the experience itself. As with most things in life, men tend to focus on the destination, but women focus on the journey.

Shut off the television or put down the newspaper when she comes home, and ask her how her day went. Then just listen; don't talk and don't try to fix every problem she has. Most of the time she just wants to talk about her life and know that you care. Do chores around the house without her having to ask you. I'm not one who has reason to brag about the amount of housework I do, but I do try to do the dishes every now and again when my wife is gone. Ask her periodically if she needs anything that you can do for her.

Your wife also needs to be praised by you on a daily basis. Your praise means more to her than anyone else's. She needs to be constantly reminded how important she is in the lives of her family members. Her role is often a thankless one that does not receive the accolades of our culture. Her maternal role as nurturer and helpmate provides vital support to your role as provider and leader of your family. If you want her to respect you and graciously submit to your leadership in the home, you need to ensure that she feels good about living up to her God-given roles in life.

Ways to Honor Your Wife

1. Always speak highly of her in front of others—even (or especially) when she's not around.
2. Express your love in public by holding her hand, walking next to her while shopping, having her walk on the inside of the sidewalk, and always opening all doors for her—even the car door. Chivalry is not dead, gentlemen.
3. Brag about her in front of your kids. Frequently thank her for the things she does for all of you in the family. Let her know she's appreciated.
4. Send her gifts at her work or in front of her friends.
5. Leave notes in unexpected places that let her know you think about her when she's not around.
6. Treat her with respect as an equal. Validate her thoughts and opinions. Listen to her. Apologize and ask forgiveness when you are wrong.
7. Do *not* let your kids be disrespectful to her—ever!

When you married your wife, you entered into a contract or covenant with her. You gave her your word that you would honor, cherish, and love her. Because of that promise, she gladly took your name. But your name is only as good as your word. Some men can walk into a bank and get a large loan solely on the basis of their good name—because they are known as men of character. If you enter into a contract with another man, that contract is only as good as his character.

Your contract with your wife is only as good as your character. If you're not a man of honor and integrity, why would your wife want to be burdened with your name? A man who does not honor his word to his wife and family causes them to lose respect for him and to not value his name.

Another way you can help meet her need for security is in the area of finances. Your wife might be more knowledgeable and efficient at paying the bills and maintaining the budget than you are, but this area is still a responsibility you should share. Men should not be apathetic (as many are in this issue) and just dump this additional burden on their wives. Part of a man's having vision and being in a leadership position in his home is knowing where his family stands financially. When a man abdicates this responsibility totally to his wife, it allows him to use her as an excuse or even blame her when things aren't going smoothly financially. It puts undue pressure on her. I feel it is honoring to her to not subject her to this additional stress on top of all the other things she does on an everyday basis. Let's admit it: men tend to be lazy and think they only have to work, but we need to be involved in more aspects of home life than just coming home and watching the football game.

Financially speaking, one of the most valuable ways to say I love you to your wife is to act responsibly with regard to debt. This may at times require you to say no to purchases that can't be paid for with cash. Debt is an epidemic in this country, and unfortunately, Christians are not immune from catching "creditfluenza." Paying credit card bills on time and managing debt according to God's Word can protect your marriage from worry and stress.

Most men are pretty good at accepting their role as providers. Where we fail more often is by overdoing that role. Oftentimes we get absorbed in our work or become obsessed with making a big income. Part of responsibly fulfilling your obligation as a provider is to have a consistent income. How much you make doesn't matter as much as the fact that you have a steady income and have budgeted it responsibly.

Also make sure you have taken steps to provide for your wife's financial security should something happen to you. An adequate savings plan for retirement as well as a life insurance policy are steps you should take after marriage, or certainly after your children are born. Make sure you have your estate in order with an executed will at an early age. Unfortunately, we never know when the time to meet our

Financial Checklist

Think about these items to determine the financial security you've prepared for your wife:

1. Do you have a will prepared? Who would raise your children should something happen to both you and your wife? Keep one copy of your will with your attorney and one in a secure place such as a safety deposit box. Designate someone as an executor of your will.
2. Do you have adequate health and disability income insurance coverage for your family?
3. Do you have adequate life insurance coverage? Experts say the amount of your life insurance should equal at least five to ten years of your annual income.
4. Where are your important papers and a letter of instruction? The letter should list the location of items such as your will, your birth certificate, the titles to your cars, house mortgage papers, military papers, and employer benefits. The letter should also contain instructions about the type of service you want, contributions in lieu of flowers, whom to contact to cancel credit cards, and general thoughts on big-picture financial items such as whether or not to pay off the mortgage. Does your wife know where your important documents such as wills and life insurance policies are kept? What about keys to safety deposit boxes? Does she have the names and telephone numbers of your attorney and accountant? While it may seem like a lot of work now, your wife will view it as a love letter if the time comes when she needs it.
5. Do you have an adequate monthly savings plan? Are you setting aside enough money to provide for your retirement needs as a couple? Do you have savings to pay for unexpected emergencies? Do you have funds for your children's college tuition?

Maker might come. Not having your estate in order to help save your family that additional burden upon your death is irresponsible at best. Making these financial preparations fulfills your wife's need for security and shows her how much you cherish her.

Modeling Love

Bill Bright, founder of Campus Crusade, said, "If a woman is beautiful in her teens and twenties, it's because God made her that way. But after she's married and the years pass, if she's still beautiful when she's fifty, sixty, and seventy years old, it's because of the way her husband treats her. So, men, take another look at your wife. If for some reason she is dowdy and glum and depressed and discouraged, look in the mirror, and see who is the major contributor to her looks. Then cultivate her with love. Before long that dull countenance will become radiant and filled with joy."[3]

Tell your wife you love her every day, and spend time praising her for her good attributes. Tell her you appreciate her when she does something for you. Don't just comment when she disappoints you. Look for opportunities to use the power God has given you to lift her up to be the utmost God intended her to be—it's probably the most profitable investment you can make with your time. You will never out-love your wife. Women are like faith. For each small mustard seed of faith you generate, God returns to you blessings hundredfold. So too a woman returns her husband's mustard seeds of love a hundredfold.

Your wife is also your greatest asset in fathering. She can build you up in front of the children, edifying you and gaining you respect that you couldn't garner on your own. When she shows you respect and actively acknowledges your leadership, you can bet your children will as well. But if she is contemptuous toward you, your children will probably not have much respect for you. She can also keep you up to speed on emotional challenges your kids are facing that you might not be aware of. Lastly, she is an excellent barometer to help you gauge how well you are doing as a father.

Your marriage does not belong to you; it belongs to God. "'I hate divorce,' says the LORD" (Mal. 2:16). Make a covenant with yourself, your wife, and God that divorce is not an option, no matter how hard your marital struggles become. After all, God specifically chose this woman to be the mother of your children and your lifelong helpmate. Then make sure you tell your children that you will never leave them. They need to hear those words spoken.

Dennis Rainey talks about a report he once saw that was written by an eleven-year-old boy, describing his home. The boy said, "My mother keeps a cookie jar and we can help ourselves, except we can't if it's too close to mealtime. Only Dad can anytime. When he comes from the office, he helps himself no matter if it is just before we eat. He always slaps my mother on the behind and brags about how great she is and how great she can cook. Then she turns around and they hug. The way they do it, you'd think they just got married or something."

Now listen to what the boy says as he concludes: "It makes me feel good. This is what I like best about my family."[4]

When my kids were little, anytime my wife and I would have an argument, they would run and hide because they were scared. Their greatest fear was that their world would be destroyed through divorce like many of their classmates' had been. Conversely, whenever my wife and I would hug and kiss, kids and even the dog would come out of the woodwork to try to worm in between us. The vibrations our love sent out were palpable throughout the house and drew kids like shoes to a mud puddle. Now, with teenagers everywhere, we enjoy "grossing them out" by kissing and slow dancing in front of them. They pretend to be disgusted, but they never seem to leave the room.

You've heard that children care more that their parents love each other than that they love them, and this is why: it's the assurance that there is something grand and good going on that doesn't rest on your shoulders, something that doesn't even culminate in you but rather invites you up into it.[5]

How do your children feel about your marriage? Are they afraid their world is about to be destroyed, or are they happy and content?

By the way, would you die for your wife and children? I would, and I think most men would be willing to sacrifice themselves for the sake of their family. But have you told your wife and children that you'd die for them? That's very powerful—to know that someone cares enough for you to die for you. I'd feel honored to know someone would die for me. I encourage you to confess that to your family. They need to know.

The Grass Is Always Greener

Unfortunately, I struggle with the same problem that most men have. I confess that sometimes I fall into the terrible habit of comparing my wife to other men's wives or even other women in general. This, of course, breaks at least one of the Ten Commandments—namely, not to covet (your neighbor's wife). It's also committing at least three of the seven deadly sins: pride, envy, and lust. Your son will probably grow up with the same tendency as well if you don't prepare him for its dangers.

I want you to understand me very clearly: I have a beautiful, loving wife whom I love dearly and would not trade for anything in the world. Truth be told, she is out of my league, and I'm lucky to have her. But my human sin nature and my "grass is always greener" mentality sometimes get the upper hand. For instance, I might see attractive women with their husbands at church and grouse to myself, "How come he has such an attractive wife? What's he got that I don't have?" This goes on ad nauseam until I take control of my thoughts.

I discipline myself to capture those thoughts, saying to myself, "My wife is beautiful. She was chosen for me by God. Without her, I would be miserable. In all likelihood, those other women have character traits that would drive me crazy—or, more than likely, they wouldn't put up with all my flaws."

Nothing positive is ever gained by comparing your wife to other women. It's an easy but very destructive habit to fall into, and one that eventually sours your relationship. Concentrate instead on your wife's positive qualities. Encourage her and treat her with honor at every opportunity. Your son is watching your every move, learning how to love a woman.

Here's one action I've found to be very helpful in keeping a proper perspective about the value of my wife. Every night in bed, after I put my book down, I turn out my light and roll over to "spoon" my wife. Just before falling asleep, the last thing I do is say a prayer to God. I whisper, "Heavenly Father, thank you for blessing me with the wife and children you have entrusted to my care. Please help me to be the kind of man, husband, and father you would have me to be. Give me the wisdom and character to be the godly leader they need." My last thoughts as I fall off to sleep are on the value of my wife and the responsibility I have as a leader in our home.

Be conscious of the fact that your son needs to learn how to love a woman. The respect, love, and honor you give your wife will determine how he will treat the women in his life forevermore. You are his main example. Make sure you teach him, through your actions, that God would have us love our wives by honoring them as Christ loves the church.

Questions for Reflection and Discussion

1. In what ways do you currently show honor and respect to your wife? Write down a list of new ways that you can begin to honor your wife.
2. Ask your wife what her five greatest needs are. Then compare and discuss them with the other men in your study group.

3. What are some ways that you can model to your son how a man should love a woman? Ask your son if he is confident that you have a good marriage and that you will never leave him. Discuss with him why he might feel this is important.

9

Respect

When people do not respect us we are sharply offended; yet deep down in his private heart no man much respects himself.

Mark Twain, *Following the Equator*

THE HERO OF this book reminds me of you." My wife's words echoed throughout my head and my heart. We had both just read an action adventure novel in which the protagonist overcame great odds. Wow! I don't think she thought much about it, but to me her comment was like showering me with love—she admired and respected me! And at least by my interpretation of her comment, she considered me a hero. I believed the story's protagonist to be a man's man—competent, strong, tough, and able to solve any problem through action and perseverance.

From twenty-three years of marriage, I can vividly remember two things Suzanne has said to me. That was the first.

The second occurred about three years ago. I was asked to go onstage at our church with my family and give my testimony during each of eight Easter weekend services. After it was all over, Suzanne and I were talking about our weekend's experiences. Suzanne offhandedly said, "I'm so proud of you. All the other women in church were looking at me and wishing it was their husband onstage." I know she didn't understand the power of that statement. But the catch in her voice conveyed her excitement to me. I was ready to climb the Empire State Building for her. She could have asked me for anything at that moment, and I would have killed myself trying to get it for her. My wife was proud of me—she respected me.

Men require admiration and respect even more than they do love. As a man, I like being loved, but what I really crave from my wife and children (especially my wife) is respect.

An old saying goes, "In order to get respect, you have to earn it." But in order to give respect or even earn it, you first must have respect for yourself. Unfortunately, self-respect is acquired by receiving it from others whose opinion you value. It's sort of a catch-22 situation, like a dog chasing his tail in a circle, round and round until he collapses from exhaustion.

Being respectful toward people does not mean being scared of or subservient toward them. It merely means treating them as you would like to be treated and extending to them the dignity each human being inherently deserves as one of God's creations.

I believe you get respect by treating others with respect. Yes, many times people behave in a manner not deserving of respect, but I think respect is a fundamental need of human beings. Once their need for it is met, they more easily offer it back. When you offer respect to someone, especially someone who looks up to you, you help develop in them a strong sense of self-respect.

Self-Respect

Just before I accepted Jesus Christ as my Savior, I was at the point where I couldn't even look myself in the eye in the mirror when I shaved in the morning. I despised what I had become. Even though I was a decent enough fellow and what our society would consider "successful," I was miserable. I had stopped dreaming about life. The more I accomplished, the less gratifying it was. I had no friends. It was me against the world, and I was going to win no matter the cost. I believed that *I* controlled my destiny and that all I needed to do was work harder and smarter to achieve my dreams and goals. Even though I'd been through years of counseling, I still didn't really respect myself. I was a good man, but I just couldn't forgive myself for the things I'd done and for not being able to live up to the standards I'd set for myself.

But when I submitted myself to Christ, God forgave my sins and past transgressions. Knowing God forgave me when I couldn't allowed me to love and respect myself. Loving myself allowed me to love my wife and children fully. Obtaining self-respect allowed me to treat my loved ones with respect. They now have what they deserve—a loving, caring husband and father who is interested in helping them be everything they can, someone to lift them up instead of a man self-absorbed in his own needs and self-pity.

Your boy needs to respect himself. He can get this by knowing that you respect him. Often we need to have a healthy sense of self-respect before we can give it to our sons.

So how does a man who does not respect himself (due to either his past transgressions or someone else's opinion of him) develop self-respect? First, I found God's forgiveness and grace to be the most important factors. Once I understood and believed in his love for me, I felt like a giant weight had been removed from my back. Reaching out to make new friends who could help me learn and hold me accountable was a big factor as well. These relationships also helped me to understand that I was not alone in my fears and concerns—that most men felt the same way I did. As I stepped out of my comfort zone to do things to grow in Christ and honor God, I garnered the respect of these men and others. Praying often for God to help me like and even love myself as he did also helped. Lastly, reading God's Word and books by other godly men helped me understand many of the issues I faced as a husband and father and gave me knowledge and self-confidence to face those issues courageously. Successfully tackling some of these issues planted and nurtured the seeds of self-respect.

This was not an overnight process, but gradually and steadily, I found myself starting to respect—even like—myself.

Giving Your Son Self-Respect

Since self-respect is developed by receiving respect from someone you admire (in my case it was God), you as a father are a natural to develop self-respect in your son. He looks up to you like no one else in this world. By showing your son respect, you have the power to ensure that he respects himself.

To show respect to someone means you consider them worthy of high regard. Peter says that we are to "show proper respect to everyone" (1 Peter 2:17) because every human bears the image of God. This includes our sons.

Make sure your boy feels good about himself. Make sure he knows you like him and are glad he is your son. No matter what trials he faces in the world, he should be able to come home and, by his father's blessings, feel that he is accepted and worthy—that he has a safe haven from the cruel world outside. You have a great power to give his life blessings from an older male to a younger male and from a father to a son.

Hold your son to high standards in conduct and character. We started a family tradition by saying, "Johnsons don't act that way." Your boy wants you to be proud of him, and he'll try to live up to the expectations you set for him. When your son does live up to those high standards, he will automatically develop self-respect.

Disrespect

As a man you value respect more than anything else in life. So does your son—after all, he's a man in training. Understand how to appropriately respect his privacy, feelings, and personal preferences without compromising his well-being.

How might your son feel if he sees you being respectful to other males outside the home and then turning around and being disrespectful to him? Ways of being disrespectful might include not considering his opinions valid, controlling all of his choices and decisions, shouting him down instead of respectfully listening to him, not allowing him to make mistakes (or overreacting when he does), humiliating him in front of his peers, or not extending him the courtesy of appropriate privacy.

In the movie *The Great Santini*, Robert Duvall plays Colonel Bull Meacham, a gung-ho Marine fighter pilot. In one powerfully disturbing scene, after Meacham's son beats him in a basketball game, Meacham follows him into the house and up the stairs, bouncing a basketball off the back of his head, all the while berating his son's manhood. It's probably the most graphic picture of a father disrespecting his son I've ever witnessed. Throughout the whole movie, Meacham never apologizes for his disrespectful and dangerous behavior as a father.

Recognize the importance of apologizing and asking for forgiveness. What better way to show respect to someone than to admit when you are wrong and ask to be forgiven? It's also a perfect example of positive leadership.

Keep in mind that as your son gets older, he needs to start having greater responsibilities. Along with that responsibility comes being treated with greater respect. If he's starting to act like a man and accepting a man's responsibilities, then he needs to be treated accordingly.

My son currently attends college during the day and works at night. Last night he came home from work at about midnight. My wife asked him to do one of his boyhood chores— the dishes. Frank said, "Mom, I just worked a ten-hour day, and now you want me to do the dishes like when I was little?" I had to admit that he was right. After Suzanne and I conferred, we told him we agreed and that perhaps the dishes could be delayed until later the next morning. Frank did voluntarily wash the dishes after Suzanne and I went to bed, but acknowledging the fact that he is starting to put away his childhood ways and giving him the respect a man deserves was important to him.

Respect for Women

One evening my daughter and I were in a local restaurant for dinner. Kelsey has turned into a gorgeous young woman. As we walked across the restaurant, I observed three males watching us from across the room. They were obviously a grandfather, a father, and his son—three generations of men all standing in a row. All three males had the same drop-jawed, glazed look on their faces as they leered at my daughter the entire length of the restaurant. My first instinct was to go over and slap all three of them. But after gaining control of myself, I recognized that here was a perfect example of the generational influence of men. The lack of respect that an older man has for women is passed down throughout the generations of his lineage. Upon further consideration, I decided I just wanted to slap the grandfather.

Boys need to be taught to respect women of all ages. They should open doors and carry heavy items for them, not because women are weaker or incapable but because they deserve to be honored and cherished.

Perhaps we need to return to a chivalric code of honor. Chivalry was a code of behavior that western European knights followed in the Middle Ages. Chivalry embodied the qualities idealized by knighthood, such as courage, justice, loyalty, nobility, faith, courtesy, honor, and gallantry toward women.

Teach your boy at a young age to open the door for his mother and sisters. As courtesy and respect manifest themselves in other areas of his life, they will become lifelong habits that will serve him well in his relationship with his future wife.

My daughter has told me several stories of high school boys being loudly flatulent during class. I'm not sure when our standards of respect for the opposite sex dropped so low. I admit I might be old-fashioned, but that action, in mixed company, doesn't seem very noble to me. I would be embarrassed to be known as the father of a boy who acted in that manner. Teach your son appropriate behavior around females, even if it's culturally acceptable to be rude and boorish.

Regarding the way we should treat women, the Bible says, "Husbands, in the same way be considerate as you live with your wives, and treat them with respect as the weaker partner and as heirs with you of the gracious gift of life, so that nothing will hinder your prayers" (1 Peter 3:7). It's interesting that Peter believed that our spiritual fellowship with God would be hindered by disregarding God's instructions concerning how we treat our wives.

We are also called upon to give our wives the ultimate in respect by loving them the same way Christ loved the church—by being willing to die for it (see Eph. 5:25). Our willingness to approach our relationship with our wives with this kind of mentality is reciprocated by their giving us respect in return. The content of both of these passages is wisdom that we need to teach our sons *before* they become husbands and fathers.

Lastly, teach your boy that respecting women means not treating them as objects for his own gratification. It also means not looking down upon them as if you are a superior being. It means recognizing their inherent worth in God's eyes as equal partners in life.

Respect for Authority

Too many people in our country are being raised without respect for authority. In order for your son to be a good leader, he has to understand how to be a good follower. Respect for authority also helps create appropriate boundaries in his life and teaches him self-discipline.

Lack of respect for authority seems to be a recent phenomenon. Certainly it seems more prevalent in our culture today than in years past. But is it really? In the book of Proverbs, a man named Agur wrote:

There is a generation that curses its father,
And does not bless its mother.
There is a generation that is pure in its own eyes,
Yet is not washed from its filthiness.
There is a generation—oh, how lofty are their eyes!
And their eyelids are lifted up.
There is a generation whose teeth are like swords,
And whose fangs are like knives,
To devour the poor from off the earth,
And the needy from among men.

Proverbs 30:11–14 NKJV

Sounds a lot like our current world, doesn't it? But Agur wrote about a generation plagued by social ills such as greed, selfishness, and lack of respect for parents sometime around 700 BC. Ironically, such evils have plagued every generation before his and since.

The apostle Paul says that to be a leader, a man must manage his family well so that his children obey him with proper respect (see 1 Tim. 3:4). Teaching your son to respect all forms of authority, especially the authority of God, gives him the gift of accountability in his life.

Your son will be subject to numerous authority figures, his parents and law enforcement personnel being the most obvious. Other figures he'll encounter as he grows include teachers and school employees, other parents, medical personnel, firefighters, coaches, public employees, civic leaders, and his boss.

This brings up some interesting questions: Does God call us to respect all authority in all circumstances? What if the authority figure is abusive, immoral, or otherwise unworthy of respect? Is respect the same as obedience? Where do you draw the line to make the difference between creating a boy who is a milquetoast, swayed by any and all prevailing opinions, and creating one who boldly follows God's Word?

To answer these questions, let's look at what God says about obeying authority figures.

In the book of Romans, Paul says,

> Everyone must submit himself to the governing authorities, for there is no authority except that which God has established. The authorities that exist have been established by God. Consequently, he who rebels against the authority is rebelling against what God has instituted, and those who do so will bring judgment upon themselves. . . . Therefore, it is necessary to submit to the authorities, not only because of possible punishment but also because of conscience.
>
> Romans 13:1–2, 5

He also exhorts Titus to "remind the people to be subject to rulers and authorities, to be obedient, to be ready to do whatever is good" (Titus 3:1).

Paul seems pretty unequivocal here about telling the early church to submit to governmental authority. Does this passage still apply to us today? What if our government condones acts that we believe are immoral or even sacrilegious—things like placing restrictions on public prayer, allowing abortion, or embracing homosexuality? Are we to submit to the will of governmental authority in issues that would appear to contradict our core values and the Bible's teachings?

The answer is yes, unless it explicitly goes against God's commands. Clearly Paul is saying that these authorities have been ordained by God's will. Every believer is to be subject to these various authorities, even if these authorities are evil like Nero, the emperor of Rome who cruelly persecuted Christians. And believers must obey government not only because it is their civic duty but also because it is their spiritual duty before God.

The author of Hebrews, in speaking about our spiritual leaders, says, "Obey your leaders and submit to their authority" (Heb. 13:17). Our spiritual leaders and teachers are judged by a higher standard by God and will be held accountable. Therefore, our duty is to submit to their authority.

Having said this, let me note that God requires us to refrain from blindly following leaders or self-imposed authorities who would have us go against God's Word. However, if an authority figure instructs us to do something wrong, we can still honor that person and their "office" without necessarily obeying them. We accomplish this by being courteous and respectful while disobeying and possibly finding an alternative option. However, righteous disobedience may carry a price. If we must disobey in order to keep from violating our convictions, then the consequences are part of the cost of following Christ.

In the United States, we have been blessed with options in nearly every situation in which we find ourselves. If we are not happy with someone in authority, we have the freedom to change that authority. Most notably, we have the option of voting many of our governmental authorities out of office in favor of someone more acceptable. We can also change employers, change schools, and change churches. We can even change our citizenship and become part of another nation. But wherever we go, we will be under some form of authority.

Learning to understand, respect, and deal with the various forms of authority your son encounters will help him recognize God's authority over his own life. When he acknowledges that authority, he can begin the process of becoming a noble man worthy of leading a family.

Boundaries

Boys need strong boundaries, so set acceptable boundaries on your son's behavior. Much like teaching discipline, creating boundaries for your son is a way of civilizing him. As Dr. James Dobson says in *Bringing Up Boys*, "A stream without banks becomes a swamp. It is your job as parents to build the channel in which the stream will run."[1]

These boundaries may need to be quite tight when your son is young, gradually loosening and expanding with age and maturity. By the time he gets ready to leave home, he should be making nearly all of the decisions governing his life with minimal input from you. The folly of sending our children away to college before they are prepared to make adult decisions is what leads to life-altering mistakes.

Realize also that by the time your children reach a certain age, they live in your home by mutual consent, not because they have to. When they are teenagers, you really cannot *force* them to do anything. They do what you want either because they respect you or because they fear you. But it's best if they acquiesce to your wishes because they respect you. If they fear you, before long they will rebel in ways that may make both of you miserable. But if you can show them that the boundaries you set for them are for their own safety and long-term best interests and not because you are some arbitrary dictator, they will respect you and *want* to obey you.

Periodically review the boundaries you've established for your son and see if they need to be loosened in order to help him learn decision-making skills. Several times recently Suzanne has questioned me about the wisdom of allowing Frank to do something new. Her natural protectiveness of her child is still in full force even though he's nearly a man. When she says with that certain air of disapproval, "Why did you let him do that?" my response is typically something like, "He's eighteen now. I couldn't stop him if he really wanted to do it anyway. We've discussed it, and he understands the dangers and ramifications involved." I'd rather have him take some risks now while he's at home than start after he's gone and has no safety net to catch him.

Frank understands that as long as he lives under our roof, he must live by our rules. In addition, the risks I allow him to take are not ones of an immoral nature. But at his age, he needs to be making the decisions that govern his life, whether I agree or disagree with them. If he never makes decisions, especially those that end in mistakes, how can he ever learn from them?

Your son's walk through life will be much easier and smoother if he respects himself and others, especially the ones he loves. Once your boy understands the concept of respect, he can use it as one of the training steps for becoming a noble man.

Questions for Reflection and Discussion

1. In what ways do you give your son the respect he deserves as a man in training?
2. What are some ways you can teach your son to respect women?
3. Does the behavior you model encourage or discourage your son from respecting other authority figures in his life?

10

Sex

With her flattering lips she seduced him.
Immediately he went after her, as an ox goes to the
slaughter.

Proverbs 7:21–22 NKJV

T HIS PASSAGE FROM Proverbs rings truer than most of us would like to admit. I would like to think I am beyond such nonsense, but the truth is, it probably wouldn't take much more than an attractive woman flattering me and before long, without some form of accountability in place, I'd blindly be following along behind her into sexual sin. Therefore, it's a good thing that (a) God made women more relationship oriented than men, (b) God does not put us in situations beyond what we can endure, and (c) the majority of women do not find me irresistible.

Now, before some of you out there start sputtering about how lacking in self-control or spiritually immature I must be for admitting that, let's be honest with ourselves, shall we? Most of you men reading this know in your hearts that you're no better than I am in this regard. We can easily say we wouldn't fall into temptation when we've never had to experience its full frontal assault. Not many of us are beyond succumbing to temptation in this area. Our male egos rationalize this kind of behavior. I cannot tell you how many godly men—men who seemed bulletproof from sexual temptation—I've observed over the years who have been forced to resign their positions as pastors, elders, or other leaders in the church because of some sexual impropriety. And that's just here in my little corner of the world! Whenever I see that happen, I always think, *But for the grace of God, there goes any one of us.*

God created men as physical, visually oriented, sexual beings. He created our sexuality with our wives to be a wonderful, exciting experience to be treasured. Unfortunately, our sexual urges have been twisted (due to our sin nature) into something beyond what God intended. Lust is a constant struggle, and those males who choose to live a life of sexual purity face a mighty battle. But through God's grace we can overcome the struggle and guilt, finding joy in our sexuality.

As with most things in life, men and women tend to view sex from differing perspectives. God created both genders as sexual beings—yet different. You and I both know that if women knew what men really think about most of the time, they quite possibly would refuse to be in the same room with us. They'd think we're perverted. And if you remember your adolescence, you'll realize that your son is probably no different than you. We tend to think our kids are different than we were at their age, but if anything, kids nowadays are probably much more worldly and sophisticated than we were.

If sex is not the first thing on a man's mind, it's certainly always lurking around in the background waiting to spring forward and pounce. Let's look at some of the minefields you and your son face every day.

Minefields

One of the challenges we face is everyday life and the circumstances we find ourselves in. One of the best strategies we can use to keep our sexual perspective intact is to not allow ourselves to be caught in situations where we might be compelled to compromise our integrity. While keeping yourself out of situations where you would be tempted is best, sometimes that's not always practical or even possible. Obviously we should stay away from topless bars, Internet pornography sites, and girlie magazines. When we are out of town on business trips, we should stay out of bars, not have dinner alone with female coworkers, and definitely not watch adult movies in our rooms. But what about the everyday circumstances of life? Suppose your office has an attractive secretary. Does that mean you should quit your job so you're not tempted by your desires? What if your child's teacher is a real stunner? Does that mean you should never talk to her about your child's progress for fear of having lust enter your heart? What about attractive women in church? Do you run from them to keep from having uncomfortable feelings? No. You learn to control your feelings and emotions to prevent acting out your desires. It's part of having a responsible masculine sexuality.

I try to work out at the gym faithfully three times a week. I participate in a grueling, hour-long, coed weight lifting class. Many of the women in the class are young and attractive. Most are in very good physical condition. The powerful struggle to control my eyes and imagination when attractive women (wearing tight, skimpy exercise clothing) are exercising around me is often greater than the physical workout itself. Thankfully, the workout is so painful that I seldom have the inclination or energy left for daydreaming. Should I not go to the gym because attractive women in skimpy clothing frequent there?

I'm presenting the above scenario a bit tongue in cheek, but my point is that all good men have learned to control their natural desires in everyday circumstances. Our sons need to learn at an early age that they too will have to responsibly master this burden as well.

When I think of my own struggle with sexual lust, I often think of Samson, whose story is told in chapters 13 through 16 of the book of Judges. Samson was set apart and equipped by God—like most men.

Samson was specially equipped to be a mighty vessel for God. Some men probably wonder if they could even defend themselves in a fight if push came to shove. But Samson didn't have that problem. God's power was manifested in Samson as superhuman strength. As you probably remember, in a fit of rage, with revenge on his mind, he picked up the jawbone of a donkey and killed a thousand men (see Judges 15). Talk about an action hero!

You know the rest of the story. As you fast-forward through Samson's escapades, you see pride, arrogance, self-centeredness, sexual immorality, disobedience, and revenge. In the end he paid with his life.

But the main thing that comes to mind when I think of Samson is sexual immorality. When I read the story of Samson, I find myself thinking, *Are you really that stupid? Wake up!* First, he goes to the Philistines looking for a wife when his parents advised against it. Then he sleeps with a prostitute. Finally, he goes to Delilah time and again, totally self-focused and self-reliant rather than God-reliant. But then I look at myself. How often do I do my own thing, beg for forgiveness, and then, seeing that I have survived, go right back to the very thing that would take my life?

Sexual sin taints everything around it. Your sexual sin impacts your family in ways you may never know. The most obvious way is the example you set. Is your sexuality honoring and showing respect to your wife? Have you taught your son that women are not just to be used to satisfy our urges and then tossed aside? Have you taught him that women are to be protected, honored, and cherished?

Remember, the example you set, especially in this area of life, is what your son will think is normal.

Accountability

Accountability makes all the difference in the world when it comes to a man being sexually responsible. For instance, I'm careful to make sure that I have other people to whom I am accountable at every seminar I present for single moms raising boys. It's not because I am so desirable personally but because I *represent* what many of these women yearn for in life. Hence I need to take the proper precautions to ensure that I have accountability at all times so I'm not tempted to take advantage of someone's vulnerability. Men are naturally equipped to know instinctively when a woman is either vulnerable or available. Even when it's not obvious, we often can sense an opportunity. This explains why some women just seem to have men flock around them, even when they are not overtly sensuous or even necessarily very attractive.

When a man walks without accountability in his life, he tends to make up the rules as he goes—he has a tendency to justify or rationalize whatever desires his mind comes up with. I remember a frightening episode that happened a while back. Suzanne and the kids were out of town for the weekend. I was driving around alone in an unfamiliar part of town, running errands on Saturday afternoon, when I approached a strip club. Portland is known as the city with the highest number of nude bars per capita of any city in the United States. Unbidden thoughts suddenly popped into my head:

You could go in there.

No one knows you around here.

No one would recognize your car here.

Suzanne's out of town; she would never find out. No one from church would see you.

I tried vainly to capture my thoughts. Going into the club was something I did not want to do under any circumstances— I had a wife, a family, a reputation, a business, a ministry, and my soul to lose. Even so, my mind continued to poke and probe to try to find ways to justify my carnal desires.

You could go in there as an experiment, just to see if your faith is strong enough to overcome your lust. Next came the clincher: *It could be like a mission. You could go in and try to testify to those poor girls in there. You could reach out to them in faith.* Yeah, right! The only reaching out I'd be doing in there wouldn't be with faith but with dollar bills, and I knew it!

My fight to control my lustful desires became a struggle of epic proportions, all because any semblance of accountability was temporarily out of my life. Finally, I resorted to prayer, asking God to remove me from the temptation. Thankfully, the stoplight was green at the corner the club was located on and I didn't have to stop, or I might have lost that battle. In retrospect, the story is rather funny now—how my mind (or flesh) tried to use cunning and guile to persuade me against my will. Yet at the time there was nothing funny about it. I was scared stupid by the potential destruction I was capable of committing in my life.

Sex Education

Talking to your kids about sex is difficult. That's why many parents today leave the sexual education of their kids to the schools. But because it's tough is precisely why you as a father have a duty to teach your kids about sexual purity. Dads are supposed to handle the tough and unpleasant tasks in life. Sure, it's not easy talking about sex, but even the Bible is pretty straightforward when discussing sexual issues—ever read Ezekiel chapter 23? I know that chapter is merely a metaphor for Jerusalem, but talking to our children about sex is probably just about as shocking as reading these lewd sexual descriptions in the Bible.

I wasn't particularly comfortable talking about sex to my son, much less my daughter. But if you start early and can become comfortable discussing these issues before puberty sets in, you're probably the best person to introduce your son to a subject that can be either a friend or a foe throughout his lifetime. He *will* go through puberty and *will* have many questions. Wouldn't you rather your son get the answers to those questions from you than from his buddies down the street—or worse yet, from the secular entertainment industry?

In order to be able to discuss openly with your son God's vision for masculine sexuality, you'll have to develop a strong relationship. This will require *your* reaching out and making the effort to foster a closer relationship. Your son probably won't come to you and initiate discussions about sex.

An article adapted from the book *Preparing Your Son for Every Man's Battle* by Stephen Arterburn, Fred Stoeker, and Mike Yorkey addresses the subject of talking about sex with your son. Here's some of what that article had to say:

> There's an old saying that goes: "Rules without relationship equal rebellion." Dads may be good at laying down a laundry list of rules, but we're pretty poor when it comes to building

a foundation for two-way communication. That's too bad, because many of us start out with a winning relationship with our son in the early years. As he grows, however, we keep on emphasizing rules when we should be emphasizing the relationship more.

He's got questions to ask, Dad. Are you going to be the one to hear them, or will his friends get the call? Your young running back is looking for the ball. He's starting to strike out on his own. Are you, God's first-team quarterback, up to the task? To do it, you'll need a relationship, and you'll have to work to get something going. Things won't fall into place naturally.

Blam! Puberty hits, and he's got questions and you've got answers, but he's not asking yet. He doesn't feel confident enough to ask you why he can't keep his eyes off Lisa's well-developed breasts in science class—which he can't help but notice when she wears those fluorescent-colored, low-cut tube tops she likes. And what's with this wet dream stuff and this masturbation thing everyone is talking about?[1]

Sounds like what you and I went through when we were that age, doesn't it? I wish I had had a father I could have gone to for guidance and answers to those kinds of questions. Better yet, I wish I had had a father who came to me and broached the subject even if I couldn't. I just remember being very confused about girls at that age, and much of the information that was passed around between my friends ended up being false.

As a father, you have wisdom and life experience that are some of the most valuable contributions you can pass on to your children. The mistakes you've made in this area can help keep your son (or daughter) from making the same mistakes—but not if you don't share them. Yes, your teens probably do think of you as a balding, potbellied, over-the-hill old guy who's living in the past—until they need your counsel to save them from harm. One of your teen's greatest weapons is to try to make you feel ashamed and old-fashioned for sharing your knowledge of anything, but especially of sexual issues. Don't let them get away with it! Share your wisdom boldly and stand by your convictions in this area, especially as your kids become teenagers—they need it.

Pornography

Pornography is the most destructive force men and boys face today. It's irresistible primarily due to a male's visual nature. Studies have shown that pornography works in men in the same stimulation centers of the brain as cocaine and has the same addictive capabilities. Viewing pornography triggers the release of a hormone that etches erotic images in a man's mind like a developer etches an image on photographic paper. This hormone creates a "high" and causes the user to want more.

These images stay with a man for the rest of his life, desensitizing him toward women and causing him to make unfair and unrealistic comparisons. No real female can compete with the airbrushed images of women who've had professional makeup artists, hairstylists, and photographers aiding them.

When I was growing up, about the only way we could get pornography was to steal *Playboy* magazine from one of my friend's dads. By today's standards, *Playboy* is tame. Much of the programming currently on network television is more graphic in nature than anything in *Playboy* in the mid-1960s.

Today we are bombarded with a constant barrage of sexually graphic images. Everywhere we turn, sex is being shoved in our faces. Everything from Victoria's Secret advertisements to unsolicited porn website spam is in your son's face from the time he wakes up until he sleeps at night. Even department store advertisements in the newspaper and some billboard ads are quite titillating. Sex sells, and Madison Avenue is quick to push the boundaries at every opportunity in order to get our money. If that requires addicting a whole generation of boys to pornography at a young age, so be it.

The reality is that pornography degrades women. Pornography makes victims of both the viewer and the viewee—the only ones who profit are those who sell it. It turns women into objects to be played with, property to be bought and sold. It makes the user think women like rape, torture, and humiliation. It allows us to use women for our own sexual gratification without the responsibility or accountability of thinking of them as real human beings.

Porn also diminishes sexual fulfillment in men. That causes discontent in our sex lives with our wives—no real woman can compete with our imagination. It breeds discontent in our lives on many levels. Porn users need bigger prizes, need more degrading, more graphic, and more explicit images. Once pornography gets its hooks in a man, it is an extremely hard addiction to break. It must be a nearly irresistible temptation for young men who are in full-blown adolescence.

The many times I've cautioned my son and other boys about the dangers of pornography, I've tried to put it in its proper perspective. Regardless of what the women involved may say, they *are* victims of this industry. Many are hooked on drugs (intentionally or unintentionally) and must do these acts to feed their habit. Many are young girls who have run away from home and been coerced or forced under threat of physical harm to perform. When you watch pornography, you are contributing to the oppression of these girls. The women involved in those pictures and videos are someone's daughters and sisters. Someday they might be some child's mother. Would your son like men lusting over and fantasizing about his sister or mother like he does the women in the porn? Guys, the next time you're tempted to look at unsavory material, think about how you'd feel if that was your daughter on camera.

Also, by viewing this material, a male is not exercising self-restraint or control. If he can't use self-control in one area of his life, he'll lack it in other areas as well. Boys who learn to govern their sexual urges grow up to be men who are able to engage in healthy sexual relations and are able to control other areas of their lives.

Lastly, pornography devalues a man's wedding vows, causing him to live in continual adultery. This applies even if he's not married. Jesus says in Matthew 5:28, "Anyone who looks on a woman to lust for her commits adultery with her in his heart" (author's paraphrase). Pornography is sin. It destroys our relationship with God. The good news is that a man can find cleansing and forgiveness from pornography through God's grace.

Pornography affects us all. A *Christianity Today* Leadership Survey in December 2001 showed that *four out of ten* pastors and 67 percent of laymen in the church regularly view pornography on the Internet.[2] Your son can access free pornography any time he wants, day or night. So guard your computer and television jealously. Use Internet protection software on your computer, and program the cable parental controls on your television to block channels boys shouldn't be watching. Don't think, *My son is too young or innocent to look at porn.* You know he would because you struggle so mightily with it yourself.

Help protect your son from this scourge of manhood; err on the side of caution in this area. Ask your wife to help hold you and your son accountable in this area. And for heaven's sake, please talk to your son often about the lifelong dangers of pornography.

Masturbation

Why is masturbation so difficult to talk about? It's not like every one of us isn't intimately familiar with the subject—some more familiar than we'd like to admit, even.

Anyone over the age of forty remembers being raised with the admonition that you would go blind or grow hair on your palms if you indulged in this act. That puritanical attitude, while generally laughed at today, still lingers in the back of many people's subconscious minds.

I had been struggling with trying to talk with my then ten-year-old son about sex in general and masturbation in particular. As Frank and I were returning from his first Boy Scout camping trip, the perfect opportunity presented itself. Frank was required to read the first few pages of the Scout's handbook with his father. These pages discussed protecting yourself from sexual molestation and abuse. As my son read these pages aloud, it gave rise to questions and opened the door to discussions that made the job of introducing him to his impending sexuality all that much easier.

Let's be up front about this. Frequent masturbation by boys is normal during adolescence. An old joke says studies have shown that 98 percent of boys masturbate—and the other 2 percent lie about it. It might be an old joke, but it's one that's true. In fact, it's normal for even very young males to like to rub or touch themselves. After all, a boy's penis is a big part of his life.

I would even go so far as to say that it is virtually impossible that an adolescent male will not engage in masturbation at least periodically, despite his moral upbringing or most stringent efforts at willpower. Likely the more pressure that's put on a young man not to indulge in this act, the more he's apt to. The reason? He thinks about it all the more often.

While masturbation is certainly a private activity, excessive disapproval of this natural inclination produces an unhealthy guilt that can affect a man's sexual attitude for a lifetime. Teaching boys the value of self-control in this area without making them feel guilty is imperative.

Another sometimes unsettling occurrence in the sexual development of adolescent boys takes place in the form of nocturnal emissions. This is when a young man has a sexually graphic dream that causes him to ejaculate in his sleep. These emissions are normal and are not something he can control. These dreams act as a pressure relief valve for the sexual psyche. Your son will likely be embarrassed if not horrified when something like this happens for the first time. In addition, the first emission or two may contain blood, which can be very frightening if a boy is not prepared beforehand.

Dad, sit down and talk to your son repeatedly, *before* he gets to the age when these activities become an issue—before adolescence sets in. Prepare him for a life of sexuality with the proper perspective and an attitude of control.

Dating

At what age should boys begin dating? Many books have been written by people much wiser than myself on this subject. However, I believe the age of dating is a subjective, family-specific decision based on the teen's maturity and the level of responsibility he has shown. My son, Frank, and several of his friends, both male and female, have read Josh Harris's book *I Kissed Dating Goodbye*. That book caused each of them to make the decision to hold off on dating until at least after high school, perhaps longer. My daughter, Kelsey, upon hearing this instantly refused to read the book out of fear that she too would be "brainwashed."

Frank and his friends have decided to break into the dating scene rather cautiously, for which I am grateful (his sister says it's because they're nerds and can't find dates, but I don't think that's the issue). A large group of guys and girls from his youth group at church attend events together, allowing relationships to grow slowly while they learn about the differences between the genders—without the pressures of dating.

Some pretty clear evidence shows that the longer teenagers hold off before beginning dating, the greater the chance that they'll remain sexually pure until marriage. As each of us knows, it's a natural human response to want to achieve a greater level of satisfaction every time we do something. This is especially true during physical experiences such as with drugs or sex. If we kiss a girl on one date, we want to go a little farther each and every time. And as each barrier breaks down, going beyond that point the next time becomes morally easier.

Discuss with your son the need to make decisions about his personal behavioral boundaries *before* he's faced with a tough choice. Knowing his limitations ahead of time is easier than trying to make decisions in the "heat of battle." While you're in the backseat of a car in the throes of passion is not a good time to decide whether or not you're going to remain sexually pure. If your son has made life decisions beforehand, he's not as likely to find himself *in* a position that requires him to make difficult choices.

Dr. James Dobson, in his fantastic book and tape series for adolescents titled *Preparing for Adolescence*, talks about the importance of making those kinds of decisions beforehand and then cementing them by creating pacts with a group of friends—sort of an accountability staff. For instance, if your son decides to remain sexually pure until marriage, he needs to express his decision to a group of like-minded friends who can all make a pact together. This creates a supportive peer group and a form of accountability. If a friend sees another friend in a situation or relationship that will potentially compromise his pact, he can call him to account.

Boys and girls mature at remarkably different rates. Several years ago, I was a consultant with Junior Achievement, so I taught one hour a week in an eighth-grade class for the entire year. I observed that many of the girls' physical development was that of a typical twenty-year-old, while most of the boys were only chest high to the girls and looked about eight years old. When did girls start developing so early? I looked back at my old high school yearbook at the girls I remember as being "built." I was shocked to see that by today's standards they looked like scrawny little grade-schoolers.

I also observed these very mature girls figuratively leading these immature little boys around by the nose, playing flirting games that the boys didn't understand in the slightest. In the high school where my wife works, girls may be observed kissing their much smaller counterparts in the halls. They look like women with their pets. Many of the boys wear a panicked look, realizing they are in over their heads. Unfortunately, because of peer pressure and natural male ego, they cannot refuse the girls' advances. I remember feeling downright scared at the age of fifteen when I found myself in the backseat of a car with an aggressive girl who was more physically developed and sexually experienced than I was. My escape felt like leaping from the clutches of a lion.

While I've jokingly gibed at my teenage daughter that boys are like dogs—they run around in packs marking their territory and sniffing after females—I think younger boys are much more reluctant to engage in physical relationships than girls. Boys are unsure of how to act in a relationship, and girls scare the heck out of them. Unfortunately, television and the movies seem to equate maturity in boys with sexual experience.

Obviously, as boys mature (usually later in high school) they catch up with the girls and become the aggressors. It's their nature. Many young men, without proper guidance, will do or say anything to get into a young lady's pants. You need to be as involved in and protective of your son's sexual purity as you would your teenage daughter's. Boys need to understand that they have a responsibility in physical relationships—it's not just the girl's job to say no.

Sexual Purity

Once upon a time a young man named Jacob went on a journey to find a wife (see Genesis 29). Upon arriving at his uncle's farm, he spied a beautiful, dark-eyed, raven-haired young shepherdess and instantly fell in love with her. The young woman's name was Rachel, and she was the youngest and most radiant daughter of Jacob's uncle. Because of his love for Rachel, Jacob agreed to work for his uncle for seven years for the privilege of marrying her. The seven years of servitude flew by, seeming like days because of his great love for her. At the end of his service, Jacob came to collect his payment of Rachel, but his uncle deceived him, substituting her older sister, Leah, in Rachel's place on the wedding night. The next morning when Jacob discovered the deception and objected, his uncle told him that their custom was that the younger sister's hand was never given in marriage before the older sister's. Therefore, Jacob agreed to work for his uncle for another seven years for the privilege of at last marrying Rachel. When he finally got his wish and made her his bride, he was so happy that he volunteered for another seven years of servitude.

This story from the Bible serves as a valuable lesson for young men. Michael Gurian says:

It inspires us to teach loyalty to adolescent males, to teach them to value above all else their responsibilities to those people whom they touch with their lips, their penises, their hearts. It propels us to teach them to earn love by working for it, even if working for it means working hard for seven years to develop emotional integrity, good communication skills, good conflict skills. It provokes us to teach them loyalty to the extended family. A male who learns responsibility to extended family in his own bloodline is more likely to form emotional bonds with his spouse's.[3]

Jacob's delayed gratification in mating with Rachel only made his love for her grow stronger and more solid as the years flew by. As part of the natural maturation process, young men who are forced (or better yet, voluntarily make the choice) to wait to satisfy their sexual urges develop a number of positive qualities that don't occur when they are given easy and early sexual gratification. Some of these growth patterns are on a physiological level, and some are on a psychological level. The main point, though, is that young men who are forced to wait develop quality character traits.

Part of our role as parents is to protect teenagers from sex until they can acquire the skills of adulthood and take on the responsibilities of marriage and parenthood.

One of the things I've noticed over the years is that my son takes his cues on how to relate sexually from me. My son always watches me to see my reaction to a beautiful woman. When he was young—and even now—whenever we drove past a sexy or scantily clad woman, I could feel him looking at me to see if I would follow her with my eyes or take an extended look.

Keep yourself and your son occupied—especially with physical activities. This tends to take the edge off the lustful urges and desires that all men, but especially adolescent boys, have. Part of the purpose of staying active and stimulating your mind and body is to ward off boredom. When a man is feeling challenged mentally and physically and has significance in his life, he feels secure, fulfilled, and good about himself. This leaves less time and energy for boredom and contemplation of the lack of adventure in his life. This lack of adventure is the downfall of many a male's sexual purity.

As John Eldredge says, "It's no coincidence that many men fall into an affair not for love, not even for sex, but by their own admission, for adventure."[4] Too often we use sex as a substitute cure for poor self-esteem, for boredom, or for not doing anything significant with our lives.

God holds you accountable for your son's sexual purity, like everything else. Because dealing with it is difficult, it's easy to justify putting it aside until it's too late. Remember not to neglect this important aspect of your son's character development.

Questions for Reflection and Discussion

1. Discuss with other men the area in which you have the most difficult struggle in maintaining your sexual purity. How would you feel if your son confessed struggling in that area as well?
2. Talk to your son beforehand about the changes his body will undergo as he goes through adolescence as well as those that girls will experience. Then, as he gets a little older, talk about sex, particularly about how a man guards his sexual purity in everyday situations.
3. Discuss with your wife what measures you can take as a family to keep pornography from impacting your children.

11

Role Models and Mentors

Boys become men by watching men, by stand-
ing close to men. Manhood is a ritual passed from
generation to generation with precious few spoken
instructions. Passing the torch of manhood is a frag-
ile, tedious task. If the rite of passage is successfully
completed, the boy-become-man is like an oak of
hardwood character. His shade and influence will
bless all those who are fortunate enough to lean on
him and rest under his canopy.

Preston Gillham, *Lifetime Guarantee*

BOYS LEARN TO become men from other men. Masculinity bestows masculinity. Femininity can never bestow
masculinity. John Eldredge says, "A boy learns who he is and
what he's got from a man, or the company of men. He cannot
learn it from any other place. He cannot learn it from other

boys, and he cannot learn it from the world of women."[1] This requires active intervention in a boy's life by an adult male. Without that intervention in the form of a role model, boys are like ships without rudders, tossed about whichever way the wind and waves of the culture throw them.

In her book *Between Mothers and Sons: The Making of Vital and Loving Men*, Evelyn Bassoff writes:

> When a boy has no flesh and blood men with whom to identify, he may turn to inspiration to the pitiful he-man images the popular media promote—Rambo or Conan. Or they turn to neighborhood gang leaders or criminals whose brutality they mistake for true masculinity.[2]

A boy has a void in his soul that asks, "Am I a man? How will I know?" Writing about the deepest question in a boy's heart, Eldredge again says:

> It's not a question—it's *the* question, the one every boy and man is longing to ask. Do I have what it takes? Am I powerful? Until a man *knows* he's a man he will forever be trying to prove he is one, while at the same time shrink from anything that might reveal he is not. Most men live their lives haunted by that question, or crippled by the answer they've been given.[3]

Boys need that void filled by the actions and blessings of another man. A woman can tell her son all day long that he is normal, that his body parts are the right size and shape, and he will never truly believe her. But another adult male telling him the answers to the questions deep in his heart will be readily, and with relief, believed. Robert Bly in *Iron John* says, "Only men can initiate men, as only women can initiate women. Women can change the embryo to a boy, but only men can change the boy to a man."[4]

Yes, you, dad, are the biggest factor in making that transformation possible. In his book *Man Enough*, Frank Pittmon states:

> Masculinity is supposed to be passed on from father to son. Women, no matter how wonderful, no matter how loving, can't teach it to us. If we don't have fathers, we should have grandfathers, uncles, stepfathers to raise us from boys into men. If we don't have men in our family, then our need for mentors begins early. If the males we know are the other teenage boys or the macho heroes from the movies, we may get a distorted, exaggerated concept of masculinity.[5]

One of the best movies I've seen that illustrates the need a boy has for an older male in his life is *Secondhand Lions*. In one heart-wrenching scene, Haley Joel Osment begs Robert Duvall to stay alive long enough to give him his "what every boy needs to hear to become a man" speech. He doesn't believe he can become a good man until he gets that information from an older, experienced male.

Boys who don't receive this blessing from their fathers are wounded deeply. Of course, most men I know deny they have been wounded—just as we are taught to do—but the wounds are there just the same. However, boys who spend time with their fathers or other adult males working, playing, going to ball games, or fishing receive the blessing of masculinity.

I was raised by a stepfather. I first met my biological father when I was twenty-four years old. Since then we have developed a strong father-son relationship. Last year I received a Father's Day card from my dad. Like most men, I don't normally care much for greeting cards. But this card was quite special—it grabbed me by the lapels and shook me. The card read:

Son, you're a blessing. You've always been a blessing to the family. . . . You took the Lord into your heart and have grown in His love. Now you do so much to praise Him in the way you live and in the things you do. It has been a joy to watch you grow, and this comes with so much pride in the special man you have become.

After that this reserved, taciturn man wrote, "Rick, always remember I love you and am proud of you. Dad." My dad's blessing meant so much to me, even at the age of forty-seven.

Renaissance Dads

The word *renaissance* means rebirth or revival. When used in conjunction with *men*, it usually typifies men who have become accomplished in a wide variety of endeavors in life. For instance, some of the most well-known "Renaissance men" include Michelangelo, an accomplished sculptor, painter, poet, and architect; Rene Descartes, a philosopher, scientist, and mathematician; Nicolaus Copernicus, a lawyer, tax collector, doctor, military governor, judge, vicar general of canon law, and astronomer; and the most famous Renaissance man of all, Leonardo da Vinci, a great architect, musician, engineer, scientist, mathematician, botanist, and inventor who also excelled in human anatomy. Each of these men achieved success, even became experts, in several unrelated fields.

Successful fathers need to be Renaissance men. But instead of focusing on fields of accomplishment, men now need to reawaken some of the qualities and roles that have made us important figures in the lives of our families and communities and then intentionally pass those traits on to our sons. It's time to revive the honored tradition of fathering.

Today, we need to glorify Renaissance Dads—men who have become adept at fathering and providing a positive impact on others' lives. These men act in ways that promote a positive view of masculinity and are active role models in the lives of all boys. Only by honoring this type of behavior will we create the desire for young men to follow in our footsteps.

I am a husband, father, son, brother, uncle, nephew, mentor, and friend. I am also a small business owner, a published author, a public speaker, a ministry founder and director, a basketball coach, a hunter, and a broken-down former high school athlete who still tries to run with the young dogs. I am accomplished in all these areas and professions with varying degrees of success. Does this make me a modern-day Renaissance man? Probably not, but it might qualify me as a Renaissance Dad. As we've learned throughout this book, at the very least it qualifies me as a role model, if for no other reason than by virtue of my gender. But beyond just their gender, true Renaissance Dads are also proficient at passing along the breadth of their experience to their sons. Hence, Renaissance Dads have three main qualifications: (1) their gender—only men can model manhood, (2) their proficiency in what they do as a father, and (3) their breadth of modeling for their sons.

As fathers, we are required to be versed in many different aspects of life. Provider, protector, counselor, teacher, coach, friend, mentor, handyman, psychologist, disciplinarian, nurturer, cheerleader, spiritual guide, and banker are all roles we have to play. How adept we become in those endeavors determines whether we become Renaissance Dad role models with great influence or merely shadow figures within our homes.

Confident Role Models

Probably the most important factor in a boy's becoming a *good* man is the presence of a positive male role model in his life—someone he can look up to.

Preston Gillham's quote at the beginning of this chapter emphasizes what it takes to create a productive man and in so doing identifies the impact men have on boys. Because males are visual creatures, they need to see models and examples of what a man looks like, how he should act in certain situations, and how he carries himself.

Fathering is a daunting and complex task. It's complicated by the world we live in, with its increasing expectations, tight economics, and competing pressures. Fathering is also complicated by a man's relationship with his own father, who in many cases was physically absent or emotionally distant.[6]

Further complications arise because fathering is a learned skill, one that men aren't typically born with. Without a positive role model early in life, a boy has an extremely difficult time learning how to be a man, father, or husband or even how to love his wife.

A boy needs a father who is confident as a man, feels that he belongs in the society around him, models male spiritual growth, and brings to the son's life a lot of healthy influences.[7]

How about you? Are you confident as a man and as a father? At one time I was not. Before coming to Christ I was uncomfortable and even intimidated by many situations I found myself in. Of course, I covered it with a false bravado that probably fooled only myself and more than likely just antagonized most everyone I came in contact with. Hence my effectiveness as a role model for my son was greatly reduced.

One of the toughest tasks I faced as a young father was knowing where to find information on fathering and even on manhood. The year 1986 found me anxiously awaiting the birth of our first child. My wife and I waited five years after our marriage, ostensibly because I wanted to own a home, before having a child. In reality, I think I knew in my heart I wasn't mature enough to handle the responsibilities of fatherhood. Our son was twenty days past due and, having large shoulders, became stuck in the birth canal. To my shock, the midwife just grabbed him by the head, braced her feet, and popped him out like a champagne cork. I was flushed with joy as my son welcomed life with a screaming breath. But on the way home, thoughts flashed through my mind and the cold hand of fear reached in and squeezed my bowels. *Wait a second, this is a little more than I bargained for. I don't know the first thing about being a father. What am I supposed to do now?* A sobering weight descended upon my shoulders. I knew now I was responsible for an innocent, defenseless life I had helped create. But I didn't know what to do and had no one to go to for advice.

I think most men feel this panic when faced with the responsibility of a child. Some cut and run from that panic, and some accept the responsibility. I suspect that most of the ones who run away are the ones who had that behavior modeled for them by other males early in life.

Today I find myself with a healthy level of self-confidence both as a father and as a man. Not that I don't still make plenty of mistakes in both roles—but I'm more comfortable "in my skin," as it were. What caused my growth in those two areas? Did I finally reach maturity at middle age? I think it had more to do with consistently asking God for wisdom and actively seeking knowledge wherever I could find it. I read a lot of books and attended many training courses on fathering. I also met with other men who were fathers to discuss trials we all faced as parents. I searched out older, more experienced men for their wisdom. And I looked to God's example, as the ultimate Father, for guidance.

Mentoring

Boys need role models. They need not only men to model appropriate behaviors but also men who are willing to actively mentor them. As a father, your primary responsibility to your son is to model the behaviors of positive masculinity and then provide him with the knowledge it takes to become a godly man and father through the mentoring process. Steve Farrar says, "It is my God-appointed task to ensure that my sons will be ready to lead a family. I must equip them to that end. Little boys are the hope of the next generation. They are the fathers of tomorrow. They must know who they are and what they are to do. They must see their role model in action."[8]

Boys who grow up without healthy men in their lives face serious disadvantages later on. They have to discover on their own how to become a man—a huge and frightening task. Boys who grow up fatherless and without a positive male role model often end up jobless, godless, and dangerous. Not only do they fail to understand their roles as providers and protectors of their families, but they are afraid to pursue a life of significance. Boys who don't receive male guidance are confused as to their roles in life, never finding security or satisfaction.

An important advantage a boy gains from having a male mentor is the ability to pursue the life he was meant to live. Every son wants to gain a sense of mission in life and receive permission from an older male (preferably his father) to pursue the mission—to feel strong, loving, masculine ground beneath his feet so that he will not, once he's an adult, have to say to his wife, to his children, or to strangers, "I don't know what a man is, please teach me."[9]

And such is the dilemma that many boys and young men are faced with today—the prospect of growing up never really knowing what it means to be a man or a father. Your son is truly blessed by your presence in his life. But a boy also needs other men besides his father in his life as role models.

In earlier times all men accepted the responsibility for teaching boys to become men. In fact, in biblical times the father had the responsibility to find other male mentors for his son as he got older. Michael Gurian says:

> When the father was gone, other personnel or tribe members stepped in. When the father wasn't known, other males protected and provided so the females and children were taken care of and then, when the young males as a group became "of age," mentored them through the social and emotional challenges of mature masculine life. The edict in the Old Testament that if a man is killed his brother must marry his wife, while hardly palatable in our day, was nonetheless a nurturing strategy required by a society that knew the risks of the lost father—kids running rampant, single mothers overwhelmed and unprotected, future problems for females who marry the males brought up without fathers.[10]

When God decided the time had come for another prophetic voice for the people, he told his prophet Elijah to find Elisha and make him the next prophet. Elijah did that by becoming Elisha's mentor. Initially, Elisha started out by being Elijah's servant. The mentoring process began by just spending time together. It involved just being close to the mentor on a day-to-day basis, observing how he reacted in certain situations.

Mentoring involves spending time with your son. But it's also important to reinforce your example with other positive male role models. I involved my son in activities where I knew he would be exposed to positive male role models such as Boy Scouts of America leaders, Little League and soccer coaches, and male teachers whenever possible. I did this perhaps subconsciously because I didn't feel competent as a father and wanted other men to help me in my inexperience. Nevertheless, it ended up being a blessing for my son that I instinctively chose the right thing to do.

As he got older, we also got together with a group of other men with sons Frank's age and created a Bible study group meeting once a month for a lesson and breakfast afterward. We went on camping trips, hikes, hunting trips, and other outings together. I wanted Frank to be around a variety of other men to see how they acted, what they said, and how they thought about life. That way the responsibility did not rest squarely on my shoulders to be the only positive male role model in his life.

One thing we need to remember is that nearly all situations and relationships involve mentoring to some degree. If you are a boss and have younger men working for you, you're not only their employer but also their mentor. Your responsibility goes beyond just teaching them job skills; it should involve teaching them life skills as well. Coaches and teachers have a responsibility to include life lessons in their educational activities. Boys and young men need input from a variety of sources in order to assimilate the information necessary to become healthy adult males.

Gurian says, "By this phrase [*mentor*] we mean a nurturing system, male-driven, in which discipline, morality teaching, and emotional sustenance are provided *by* males, *for* males. . . . We mean fathers, male mentors, coaches, teachers, older boys, grandfathers and other older men, male leaders, male role models, male heroes, male sports figures, and male peers."[11]

As men, not only is it our responsibility to find other men to be involved in our son's life, it is also our responsibility to be involved in other boys' lives. Children without fathers need men to step forward as positive influences in their lives. Young men without exposure to mature male leadership can become predators. Young women who have been abandoned by their fathers often try to find the paternal love and attention they desperately require in the wrong places—like the backseat of a car.

A woman from the Big Brothers Big Sisters organization came to talk to me one day. She was introducing a program called Amachi, which targets adults from faith-based organizations to mentor children who have one or both parents in prison. I told her right up front that I just did not have the time to mentor a young boy.

She proceeded to tell me that this program had been in the Portland area for only two years but already had a waiting list of 240 boys between the ages of six and twelve. Because men were so reluctant to volunteer, the average waiting period for these boys was two years! I thought, *My goodness, I can't volunteer because I just don't have the time. But, Lord, how can I not volunteer?* Two years is a lifetime for boys at that age waiting for a male role model to come into their lives, especially for ones who have recognized the need for and want a mentor in their lives. Knowing that, how could I not mentor a young boy?

The ten-year-old boy I mentor is like a dry sponge soaking up my influence. He's respectful and eager for my attention. I'm continually amazed at some of the things he has never been taught because of never having spent much time around a healthy adult male. He's also very angry, and understandably so. He would be abnormal if he weren't angry. He has been deprived of the God-given right to have an older male in his life to help guide him to manhood.

Interestingly, both his teacher and his counselor are convinced that he suffers from ADHD, yet around me he is calm and respectful.

I don't know if I can or will make any difference in the life of this boy, but I'm trying. If we don't help these boys, we are destined to have a lot of angry, out-of-control young men to contend with someday, as well as a bunch of single moms with fatherless children. Besides, I don't want to have to explain to God someday that I ignored all these boys who needed my attention just because I was more interested in my own needs and desires.

Robert Lewis says this about young men today:

> Boys under 25 in this country are approaching masculine meltdown. Because of a lack of male role models in their lives, they have no idea what a man is, how a man acts, how he feels, or what he lives for. They have no vision of what men do. And many of them are angry. Fatherless children are crippled children. In their rage against their fatherless "wounds" they often commit acts of violence. Boys without an older male involved in their lives have no accountability. They tend to drift into themselves, into a world of fantasy and isolation.[12]

Older men have a responsibility to walk alongside younger men, giving them the benefit of their experience. Likewise, young men should be open—in fact, eager—to receive advice from the more mature members of their gender. Too often, however, male pride on both sides stops them from sharing and receiving this crucial information.

Find other boys and young men to mentor; your responsibility does not stop with your son. The fact is that if we do not curb the multitude of young men entering adulthood without proper training in how to be a man, a father, and a husband, our culture will eventually implode.

Truthfully, young men today are desperately seeking older males to tell them the secrets of living life as a healthy man in today's environment. If we only knew how important we are in the lives of young men and boys, we would not be so reluctant to step in and give them the benefit of our experience.

Women make up 85 percent of single parents in our country.[13] Approximately 50 percent of the children in this country will live at least a portion of their growing-up years in a single-parent home. Today 30 percent of children are born out of wedlock. Nearly 90 percent of all violent crime is committed by men raised by single mothers. At least 70 percent of men in prison are from fatherless homes.

These statistics are not an indictment of women. They are an indictment of men. We are the ones who have dropped the ball. It's up to us as a collective gender to stop this trend and raise up a generation of men who can lead our society back into the light. As we've seen, we can accomplish this only by spending time with boys and being involved in their lives.

I know there are a myriad of reasons why a father may not be involved in his children's lives, especially after a divorce. Some of them are even very good, reasonable, and understandable excuses. I have spoken with many men whose story of divorce and the subsequent struggles broke my heart. However, that does not change the fact that without your influence, your children, especially your sons, will have nearly overwhelming obstacles to overcome if they are to lead productive, happy, and fulfilling lives. And their struggles will likely wreak havoc on those around them—especially your grandchildren. I think that's worth fighting for and even enduring some difficult circumstances—taking some of those "hits" we talked about earlier that warrior dads must endure.

I can only imagine how difficult it must be to raise and nurture another man's child. But if you are a stepfather, your role is even more important, especially if the boy's biological father is not actively involved in his life. Your stepson needs an older male to show him what it means to be a man. Boys typically have a tough time accepting and bonding with a male other than their father. This makes your task all the harder. One of the nobler things in life that I can think of is for a man to willingly raise someone else's child—provided he does the best he can, without malice or contempt.

One of the most important yet possibly most unrecognized men in history was a stepfather. I'm speaking of Joseph, step-father to Jesus. We don't read much about him in the Bible, and he seems to have disappeared sometime around Jesus's teen years. However, he played a critical role in Jesus's life and consequently in all of our lives. Joseph provided protection for the living God in human form—he saved Jesus from being killed as a baby. Joseph provided provision and mentoring to Jesus throughout his early, formative years of life. Joseph also raised other men, James and Jude, who became supporters and apostles of Jesus. Joseph played out the role that God had in store for him. It couldn't have been easy, what with Mary becoming pregnant during their engagement. What kind of scorn and peer pressure do you think Joseph faced in this situation—even after the birth of the child he took on as his own? What kind of ridicule would you be subjected to in that situation even today? Even though Joseph seems to have been undervalued and really sort of a footnote in biblical history, I suspect his contributions as a stepfather were greatly honored by God. If you are a stepfather and your boy's father is not a good role model due to alcoholism, drug addiction, philandering, irresponsibility, or any of a dozen other reasons, let your boy know he doesn't have to grow up to be like his father. In the movie *The Mighty*, the biggest fear of one of the young boys in the story was that he would turn out to be a sadistic criminal like his father. He thought that because his father was a certain way, he was destined to be that way regardless of his own wishes. Many boys do feel this way, and you should let your stepson know he does not have to automatically grow up to be like his father.

The biggest contribution you can make to a young man's life is to spend time with him. It doesn't have to be anything special; just the fact that you are spending your undivided time with him is what counts. Adults think of time in terms of quality. Kids think of time in terms of quantity. Over and over again I hear from teenagers that the one thing they want most from their father is his time—not money, not material goods, not exotic vacations—just time.

My experiences with mentoring boys through organizations such as Big Brothers Big Sisters is that these boys just want your time and attention. They don't care where you go with them or what you do, but they do desperately crave your time together. If you think that you are not important, I encourage you to become a mentor to an at-risk boy. It is a humbling experience to realize that just your very being has great value to another person. We tend to think that we are not worthy or capable of being a mentor, but that is absolutely not true. Try it—you might be surprised how capable you really are.

Heroes

Part of the mentoring process is holding up male heroes for your son; he needs to see what they look like. Heroes need not be famous, larger-than-life action figures. They can be the average guy down the street who gets up every day and goes to work at a job he hates just to support his family (say this to your son and see what his response is). Occasionally the newspaper or a magazine will have an article about a man who has lived a heroic life or committed an act of heroism. Here are some easy ways to introduce heroes (besides yourself) into your son's life.

Movies

Movies provide a resource for heroes you can use to supplement other sources. Unfortunately, today's movies providing positive male role models are few and far between. Look for movies with men who have good moral convictions and stand for strong values. Enjoy them with your boy. Have a guys' movie night with pizza and soda pop. Remember to talk about the positive character traits the heroes display and the negative ones the villains flaunt.

I still get goose bumps watching Mel Gibson as William Wallace in *Braveheart*. I am inspired every time I hear him say, "And dying in your beds, many years from now, would you be willing to trade all the days from this day to that for one chance, just one chance, to come back here and tell our enemies that they may take our lives, but they'll never take our freedom!"

In the movie *Unbreakable* starring Bruce Willis, a young boy is so convinced his father is a superhero destined to save people's lives that the father eventually becomes one despite his reluctance. The son's faith in his father empowered him to become what God had destined him to be—a valuable lesson for all men.

Here are some more inspirational "guy" movies: *Master and Commander* with Russell Crowe; *The Last Samurai* starring Tom Cruise; *The Last of the Mohicans* starring Daniel Day-Lewis; *The Patriot* starring Mel Gibson; *Remember the Titans* starring Denzel Washington; *Hoosiers* starring Gene Hackman; *Rudy* starring Sean Astin; *Secondhand Lions* with

Robert Duvall; *Lonesome Dove* with Robert Duvall; *Glory* starring Matthew Broderick; *Gladiator* starring Russell Crowe; *Signs* starring Mel Gibson; and *We Were Soldiers* with Mel Gibson. The movie *Rob Roy* with Liam Neeson, while perhaps too sexually graphic for family fare, does an incredible job of showing the best and absolute worst character traits that men possess. And as we know, any of the Lord of the Rings, Star Wars, or Indiana Jones movies are just plain fun for boys (and dads too).

I've provided at the end of this book a list of resources that includes some of my favorite movies—enjoy them!

Reading

Somehow we've allowed the myth to circulate that reading is somehow bookish and unmanly. But reading is one of the greatest pastimes I've discovered. If you're reading this book, you know there's nothing unmanly about reading. One of the greatest men in the history of our country, Abraham Lincoln, basically educated himself by reading books. I am convinced that reading is what separates people who struggle with making poor choices their entire lives from those who have hope of a brighter future. Books, even more than movies, provide a wealth of role models for your son.

Boys are typically not readers. Our culture does not do much to encourage them to be readers. Encourage your son to read; it is a wonderful gift that he will appreciate for a lifetime.

Encourage your son by letting him see you reading. Leave books lying around the house. Encourage relatives and family friends whom your son loves and admires (especially other males) to give books as presents. Get your son his own library card at an early age. Let your son make his own choices at the library or bookstore, and get involved with his interests.

For instance, if he likes music, encourage his participation in school or with an instrument.

Even if reading is an unpleasant chore for you, I urge you to give books to your son as presents—and not just one book but five or six at a time. Start at a young age; don't wait until he's seven or eight years old. Tout the merits of reading to your son, even if you don't enjoy it yourself. Model reading to your son as often as possible. Read in front of him at every opportunity, even if it's just the newspaper. At the very least, let him see you carrying the newspaper, a book, or a magazine around with you occasionally. Read stories to him when he's little. Have him read to you as he gets older.

I like to read out loud to my wife when I come across something that is particularly insightful. In fact, sometimes I will read aloud entire chapters from books we both enjoy. All the better if the kids are around. They get the benefit of hearing important information from a more credible source than just dad. Not only that, but it's not a lecture because I haven't directed it toward them. Since I'm reading to their mother, they can more objectively consider the information without the emotional rejection that accompanies a lecture.

The trick to helping your son become a reader is to find books written at a level that is not too difficult yet is sufficiently challenging to be of interest to him. If they are too hard to read, he will become discouraged. It's sort of like the first time I played catch with Frank. He was about three years old, and I wasn't smart enough to start out using a tennis ball. I used a hard ball. Of course, the first time I lobbed him the ball, it hit him smack dab in the mug. He never really liked baseball too much after that. Don't whack your son in the coconut with a "hardball" book right off the bat if you want him to enjoy reading for the rest of his life.

Remember, his books need to be adventurous, with a swashbuckling dose of action—stories you'd enjoy too. When you give a gift, give a book that goes along with it. For example, if you give him a basketball, include a book about a famous basketball player. If you give him a baseball glove, give him a book about a baseball star. Whatever his interests may be—dinosaurs, geology, insects, snakes, rodeos, animals, trains, race cars, music, or art—find a book about someone he can look up to in that arena. "Eyewitness" type of books provide a wealth of information on almost any subject along with interesting pictures and facts.

Books about our founding fathers, pioneers, frontiersmen (Davy Crockett, Daniel Boone, and Lewis and Clark), cowboys (Wild Bill Hickock, Buffalo Bill, Wyatt Earp), soldiers (all the way from ancient times to the present), explorers (Magellan, Francis Drake, De Soto, Marco Polo, Henry Hudson, Christopher Columbus, Leif Erickson), and athletes generally present good role models with the action boys like. Boys crave heroes. Biographies and autobiographies of famous men throughout history also provide wonderful opportunities to learn about the background and character traits of men who have accomplished great deeds. I can still remember as a boy reading biographies about frontiersmen like Kit Carson and Jim Bowie and sports figures such as Jim Thorpe, Glen Cunningham, and Jack Dempsey. I have been inspired throughout my life by reading of the challenges they overcame in order to succeed.

Recognize that reading for information is as legitimate as reading novels. Acknowledge this fact to your son when he follows written instructions for a hobby or reads the sports pages. Some boys love acquiring facts or trivia and especially enjoy the *Guinness Book of World Records*, the *World Almanac*, or sports almanacs just for the fun of browsing through them.

Fiction serves to stimulate a boy's imagination, creating visions of adventure and greatness while supplying him with wonderful heroes to look up to. Just a few of the thousands of good fiction books for boys are *Where the Red Fern Grows* by Wilson Rawls; *The Red Badge of Courage* by Stephen Crane; *The Jungle Book* and *Captains Courageous* by Rudyard Kipling; *Treasure Island* by Robert Lewis Stevenson; *The Adventures of Huckleberry Finn* by Mark Twain; *White Fang, Sea Wolf*, and *Call of the Wild* by Jack London; *The Hobbit* and *The Lord of the Rings* by J. R. R. Tolkien; *Robinson Crusoe* by Daniel Defoe; *The Old Man and the Sea* by Ernest Hemingway; *The Grapes of Wrath* by John Steinbeck; *The Lord of the Flies* by William Golding; *Shogun* by James Clavell; *African Queen* by C. S. Forrester; *King Solomon's Mines* by H. R. Haggard; *20,000 Leagues under the Sea* by Jules Verne; *The Lion, the Witch and the Wardrobe* by C. S. Lewis; and *Endurance* by Alfred Lansing. A number of websites and the local library generally have lists of good books for boys to read.

What Happened to All the Heroes?

Our society craves heroes yet can't wait to tear them down. Perhaps because of that mentality, we've created a generation of men reluctant to be heroes. Charles Barkley, former professional basketball player, is famous for, among other things, saying, "I am not a role model." Paul Zweig writes in his book *The Adventurer: The Fate of Adventure in the Western World*:

> By hero, we tend to mean a heightened man who, more than other men, possesses qualities of courage, loyalty, resourcefulness, charisma, above all, selflessness. He is an example of right behavior; the sort of man who risks his life to protect his society's values, sacrificing his personal needs for those of the community. Virgil's Aeneas is a hero in this sense of the word. He devotes his warrior skills, his pleasures, and finally

his life to the historical destiny of founding Rome. Dante climbing to heaven in *The Divine Comedy* is a hero. Sergeant York risking his life to "end all wars" is a hero. . . . There is, of course, another sort of heightened man who bulks large in the popular imagination. . . . He is not "loyal," not a model of right behavior. Quite the contrary, he fascinates because he undermines the expected order. He possesses the qualities of the "hero": skill, resourcefulness, courage, intelligence. But he is the opposite of selfless. He is hungry; "heightened," not . as an example, but as a presence, a phenomenon of sheer energy. One thinks of certain sports heroes, who boast and indulge their whims; who cannot be relied on, not because they are treacherous, but because the order of their needs is purely idiosyncratic.[14]

More and more the modern athlete is becoming an anti-hero of sorts. Such figures apparently enjoy the money, fame, and accolades; they just don't want the responsibility that goes along with them. Not having had heroes and role models to look up to when they grew up may very well be the reason. I recently saw an interview with Jim Brown, the great NFL running back from the 1960s. He now works with the young players on his former team, the Cleveland Browns. Brown said, "Most of the young guys on this team, while being very nice, really have little education, and most have grown up without a father. Consequently, they don't know how to handle everyday situations in life."[15]

Doesn't it sound as though we all have a responsibility to provide a model for young boys and men? Whether they like it or not, sports heroes and rock stars *are* role models. What they do and say gets emulated by boys, whether they accept it or not. These personalities can say whatever they want on television or in the newspapers about not being role models, but it doesn't change the facts. Our sons are watching. Perhaps part of the struggles young men face today are due to

217

the fact that older men have actively and even aggressively abdicated their responsibility as role models.

Your son and other boys within your sphere of influence all need your presence in order to become the men God created them to be. They need your wisdom, time, and influence and the benefit of your experience to make the successful transition from boyhood to noble manhood. In short, they need *you* to be their hero.

Questions for Reflection and Discussion

1. Think about the best male role models throughout your life. Tell your son about these men and what made them important in your life.
2. Make a list of movies and books you want your son to see and read. Talk to other men and get recommendations of their favorite inspirational movies and books.
3. Actively look for other male mentors to be involved in your son's life. Think about this question: If something should happen to you, what kind of men would you want involved in your son's life?
4. Discuss with your wife and family how you might become a mentor for other needy boys.

12

Leaving a Legacy

Plans are nothing. Planning is everything.

Dwight D. Eisenhower

THE LEGACY YOU leave on this earth depends upon the planning you put into it. Boys who have never had healthy masculinity modeled for them face an extremely difficult, if not impossible, task: becoming a good man. Since healthy masculinity is rarely modeled in the movies, on television, or in our cultural heroes, without the presence and guidance of a real man in his life, a boy will never understand how to think, act, and behave like a man. Your legacy and your son's legacy depend upon your active involvement in his life. That kind of responsibility requires planning and intentional performance so that we are not just flying by the seat of our pants.

No dying man ever wishes he'd spent more time at the office. If we're fortunate, we discover long before we're on our deathbeds the importance of our family and of passing on a legacy for the coming generations. Our culture tends to think of legacy in terms of monetary worth. But a true legacy is based on whether we stood for something, whether we made a difference in someone's life, and whether our lives will be remembered because of the quality of life we lived.

When I was a young man, I worked in a fruit cannery. One of the operations was to mash the lower-grade apples and pears into mush, cook them, separate the juice, and finally distill the liquid, capturing the "essence" of the fruit. The essence is the taste and smell of the fruit—its soul, if you will. This essence was then applied in varying concentrations to a variety of products to enhance them or to make them more appealing and palatable.

John Eldredge says, "Masculinity is an essence passed on from father to son."[1] This masculine essence, applied in varying concentrations, can make boys into healthy, noble men of all types, shapes, and sizes. Without it, they grow up to look like men but don't have the essence, or soul, of a true man.

Boys need men to teach them how the world works and to make them noble. Joseph McPherson, recently retired headmaster of The Heights School, an all-male private school in Potomac, Maryland, believes that men are essential in teaching boys about the world. Christina Hoff Sommers, in her book *The War against Boys*, characterizes McPherson's philosophy this way:

> For McPherson, the goal of educating children [boys] is not only to impart information and teach skills but to "provide them with a noble vision of life—to convey to them that they have to do something great with their lives." He believes that adult males are uniquely suited to impart this philosophy to boys. McPherson explains that male teachers can introduce boys to the world of ideas, of nature, art, poetry, and music,

and generally "expand their range of interests without the boys feeling they are risking their masculinity."[2]

Without you actively involved in your son's life, who will teach him these ideologies? Who will help him to become the man God has planned for him to be? Who will provide him with a noble vision of life and convey to him that he has to do something great with his life? These are the kind of questions that, if approached with intent and forethought, can create a legacy of masculine leadership that impacts generations of people.

Action Plan

I have observed over a long period of time that goals and accomplishments don't just happen—they require planning. An old saying goes, "We don't plan to fail; we just fail to plan."

Consider which values and character traits you want your son to demonstrate. Then design a program to help intentionally teach him those values. Think ahead of time about different situations your son is likely to find himself in. These circumstances will provide opportunities to teach him about specific character traits. When you find yourself or your son in these situations, you're then prepared to turn them into life-learning lessons instead of just watching the opportunities float by. These lessons could involve hypothetical situations or ones of a more practical nature.

For instance, as my son continues to work more hours, we are gradually increasing the amount of money he has to contribute to our household. He now pays a small amount of rent, half his car payment, half his auto insurance coverage, and some grocery money (although certainly not as much as he consumes) each month, as well as buying his own gasoline for his car. This teaches him how to budget his income to pay for the expenses he will encounter when he moves out on his own.

Next, write your plan down on paper as an outline. A goal that is not written down tends to never come to fruition. This will help you to father intentionally instead of reactively.

Have a plan, but don't fall in love with it. Be flexible enough to change it when necessary. Your plan will need to be revisited and adjusted periodically, perhaps once a year or more. Remember that as your son grows, your responses and the way you deal with him will need to change. What works when he is seven years old will likely not work when he is seventeen.

Keep Learning

Keep learning for your own benefit and as an example to your son. Many men quit learning after they leave school. When they quit learning, they quit growing. Teach your son that education is a lifelong process and those who continue to gain wisdom benefit the most. Read many books—both fiction and nonfiction. Attend seminars on a wide variety of subjects. Go back to school. The more you invest in and develop yourself, the more you can give to your son.

I feel like the older I get, the less I know. About the only thing I do know for sure is that if you wait until you're forty-five years old to start snowboarding, you'd better have a hot tub nearby. I also know that I am where I am today because I have continued to learn and grow and not stagnated in my personal development.

One of the best ways to continue to learn and gain wisdom is by remaining teachable. Men who lose their willingness to learn are destined to crash into the brick wall of life. Our old friend Samson is a good example of a man who was not teachable. John Maxwell wrote,

> Samson was so self-centered, so undisciplined, so arrogant, that he lost his teachability. And that loss can make even the most talented person ineffective as a leader. . . . Every time he faced a problem, he reacted with violence rather than deal with his character flaws.[3]

As fathers, our roles as leaders and teachers are greatly compromised when we lose our teachability and stop learning.

Develop a Vision for Your Son

Vision is what makes a man. As the visionary for our families, the ability to see the big picture is the most important attribute we possess. Yet many men squander or misplace their vision—then wonder why they lose their families. God gave you the ability to look out over the horizon and into the future. Use that gift to keep your family safe from the schemes of the enemy.

Develop a vision for your son. Always hold him to that higher standard. Yes, the narrow path is harder to walk down, and most people take the easy path through life. But easy is not always best. Your son needs to have a vision of what a man should be—hopefully modeled by you. He needs high standards to strive toward and goals and dreams to motivate him. Make sure you share your vision with him so he knows what to expect. People have a pretty hard time living up to our expectations if we never tell them what those expectations are.

As your son comes of age, take an opportunity to sit down with him and come to a joint "meeting of the minds." Have a meeting where a father and son can compare notes on what it means to be a man. This provides a good time to explain some of the changes in your relationship when your role begins to change from authoritarian to advisor. It also gives you a chance to make sure he knows the answers to some very serious questions. For instance, have you specifically talked with your son about what it means to be a man? How about what traits a man exhibits? Have you even told your boy that when he grows up his primary role in life will be to provide for and protect his family? Too many young men today grow up thinking that to be successful means to wear the right clothes, drive the right kind of car, and have the coolest friends.

Stu Weber likens men today to "rusty knights in a hostile land." He says, "I'm reminded of many of my brothers today. Modern man. Emasculated man. Just a shadow of God's intention for masculinity. Something has happened to manhood. Something has attacked its heart so that manhood is somehow less masculine."[4]

What has attacked and diminished manhood is the lack of vision for masculinity. Over the past several generations, an increasingly larger percentage of sons have been raised by fathers who either did not know what it means to be a man or didn't care enough to provide a positive model of it. Your vision for your son must clearly define what a man is and what a father does, or he is at risk of becoming one of Weber's "rusty knights."

Not only that, but as a man, you are the only one who can impart a vision of virtue and nobility upon boys. Headmaster Damon Bradley of Landon, another distinguished boys' school, wrote the following regarding the ancient view that manliness and virtue are ultimately related:

Our Latin teacher has explained to me that the Latin word for "man" (*vir*) can easily be recognized in the word *virtute*, as its root derivation, suggesting that "virtue" and "manliness" were integrally linked in the Roman mind. . . . In the classical world—and arguably in boys' schools—manliness is defined more by virtue and less by might.[5]

Our world is looking for leaders of virtue, men with vision. Proverbs 29:18 says, "Without a vision the people perish" (author's paraphrase).

For men, who are responsible for other people's lives, lack of vision is destructive, leading to whole families not reaching their full potential. Long-term vision is what separates successful men and fathers from ineffective ones. Part of a man's job is to see the bigger picture. He has to know what's ahead in order to give the appropriate warnings. That way when life gets tough, we men don't have a tendency to react instead of responding purposefully. If we can't see the whole lay of the land, we cannot guide our sons in the direction they need to go, especially when they get lost.

Prayer

The most important action you can take on your son's behalf is to pray for him on a daily basis. Prayer is the most powerful tool in the universe. God is the ultimate Father in the universe. Reading his Word faithfully, praying to him, and reaching out to other godly men will help you develop into the kind of father God would have you become. Everything you need to know to be a good husband, father, and man is contained in the Bible.

Sacrificially offer your son to God like Abraham did his son Isaac. No, I don't mean you should pray for his death, but pray for his being dedicated to the Lord. Ask the Father how you can raise your son to honor God and fulfill the destiny God has in store for him. Recognize that your son is God's child and that you have just been granted caretaker and mentor status.

Pray for wisdom daily. Proverbs 3:13 says, "Blessed is the man who finds wisdom." I cannot tell you how many times I've prayed to God for wisdom, but I know I have done it often. I have prayed for my children every day since I became a Christian.

The purpose of praying to and worshiping God is not only to determine your destiny; it is also to save your family. God has called men to deliver those closest to them.

General Douglas MacArthur said:

> By profession, I am a soldier, and I take pride in the fact, but I am prouder to be a father. A soldier destroys in order to build. The father builds, never destroys. The one has the potentialities of death, the other embodies creation and life. And while the hordes of death are mighty, the battles of life are mightier still. My hope is that my son, when I am gone, will remember me not from battle, but in the home, repeating with him the simple prayer "Our Father, which art in heaven."

Pray daily with your wife as part of praying for your son. Your wife is an incredibly effective partner and resource in helping raise your children. Your coming together as a team in this area not only effectively petitions the Lord and intercedes on your son's behalf but also sets a good example for your son and improves your relationship with your wife. Remember to pray for your wife too. Pray for her to be an effective partner in your parenting team and for her healthy relationship with your son.

Pray for your son's future: for the life he will lead, the people he will touch, and the children he will raise. And then continue to pray for him throughout his lifetime. The impact of a praying father cannot be overestimated. James

5:16 says, "The prayer of a righteous man is powerful and effective." Use that power to help create a legacy for you and your son.

Closing Thoughts

In closing this book, let me summarize my counsel about raising your son to nobility with one sentence: *remember to tell your boy you love him and are proud of him, to pray for him, to spend time with him, and to love his mother.* That's my best advice.

Good luck, good fathering, and may God bless you.

Resources

Books for Men

Arterburn, Stephen, and Fred Stoecker, with Mike Yorkey. *Every Man's Battle*. Colorado Springs: WaterBrook Press, 2000.

Blankenhorn, David. *Fatherless America*. New York: Basic Books, 1995.

Canfield, Ken. *The Heart of a Father*. Chicago: Northfield Publishing, 1996.

———. *The 7 Secrets of Effective Fathers*. Wheaton: Tyndale, 1992.

Dobson, James. *Bringing Up Boys*. Wheaton: Tyndale, 2001.

Eldredge, John. *Wild at Heart*. Nashville: Thomas Nelson, 2001.

Farrar, Steve. *Anchor Man*. Nashville: Thomas Nelson, 1998.

———. *Point Man*. Sisters, OR: Multnomah, 1990.

Gillham, Preston. *Things Only Men Know*. Eugene, OR: Harvest House, 1999.

Gurian, Michael. *A Fine Young Man*. New York: Tarcher/Putnam, 1999.

———. *The Wonder of Boys*. New York: Tarcher/Putnam, 1997.

Hughes, R. Kent. *Disciplines of a Godly Man*. Wheaton: Crossway, 1991.

Lewis, Robert. *Raising a Modern-Day Knight*. Wheaton: Tyndale, 1997.

Morley, Patrick. *The Man in the Mirror*. Grand Rapids: Zondervan, 1997.

Oliver, Gary and Carrie. *Raising Sons and Loving It!* Grand Rapids: Zondervan, 2000.

Sommers, Christina Hoff. *The War against Boys: How Misguided Feminism Is Harming Our Young Men*. New York: Simon & Schuster, 2000.

Weber, Stu. *Tender Warrior*. Sisters, OR: Multnomah, 1993.

Books for Boys

Consider reading these books to or aloud with your boy.

Burroughs, Edgar Rice. *Tarzan*.
Clavell, James. *Shogun*.
Defoe, Daniel. *Robinson Crusoe*.
Forrester, C. S. *African Queen*.
Golding, William. *The Lord of the Flies*.
Haggard, H. R. *King Solomon's Mines*.
Hemingway, Ernest. *The Old Man and the Sea*.
Kipling, Rudyard. *Captains Courageous*.
Kipling, Rudyard. *The Jungle Book*.
Lansing, Alfred. *Endurance*.
Lewis, C. S. *The Lion, the Witch and the Wardrobe*.
London, Jack. *Call of the Wild*.
London, Jack. *Sea Wolf*.
London, Jack. *White Fang*.
Rawls, Wilson. *Where the Red Fern Grows*.
Steinbeck, John. *The Grapes of Wrath*.
Stevenson, Robert Lewis. *Treasure Island*.
Tolkien, J. R. R. *The Hobbit*.
Tolkien, J. R. R. The Lord of the Rings trilogy.
Twain, Mark. *The Adventures of Huckleberry Finn*.
Verne, Jules. *20,000 Leagues under the Sea*.

Any books published before 1965 about sports heroes, pioneers, frontiersmen, soldiers, and our founding fathers usually provide good role models for boys.

Movies

Be sure to review all movies first to make sure they're appropriate for your son at his current stage of development.

Angus starring Kathy Bates
Braveheart starring Mel Gibson
Chariots of Fire starring Ben Cross
The Emperor's Club with Kevin Kline
Gladiator starring Russell Crowe

Glory starring Matthew Broderick

The Green Mile with Tom Hanks (warning: contains graphic language and prison situations)

Hoosiers starring Gene Hackman

The Indiana Jones trilogy starring Harrison Ford

The Jack Bull starring John Cusack

The Last of the Mohicans starring Daniel Day-Lewis

The Last Samurai starring Tom Cruise

Lonesome Dove with Robert Duvall

The Lord of the Rings trilogy starring Elijah Wood

Master and Commander starring Russell Crowe

The Mighty with Sharon Stone

The Mission with Robert DeNiro

Old Yeller starring Fess Parker

Open Range with Robert Duvall and Kevin Costner

Patriot starring Mel Gibson

Pay It Forward starring Haley Joel Osment

The Princess Bride starring Carey Elwes

Radio with Ed Harris

Remember the Titans starring Denzel Washington

Rob Roy starring Liam Neeson (warning: this movie, while presenting some very strong masculine values, also has several extremely graphic scenes and should be previewed first to determine if your son is mature enough to watch it—this film may not be suitable for family fare)

The Rookie with Dennis Quaid

Rudy starring Sean Astin

Scent of a Woman with Al Pacino

Schindler's List starring Liam Neeson (warning: contains graphic violence)

Secondhand Lions with Robert Duvall

Signs starring Mel Gibson

Simon Birch with Ashley Judd

The Star Wars trilogy starring Mark Hamill and Harrison Ford

To Kill a Mockingbird starring Gregory Peck

Unbreakable starring Bruce Willis

We Were Soldiers with Mel Gibson

White Squall with Jeff Bridges

Notes

Chapter 2: Authentic Fatherhood

1. Frank Pittmon, *Fathers, Sons and the Search for Masculinity* (New York: Berkeley Publishing Group, 1993), 274.

2. James C. Dobson, *Straight Talk to Men and Their Wives* (Waco: Word, 1980), 21.

3. Stu Weber, *Tender Warrior* (Sisters, OR: Multnomah, 1993), 145.

4. Ibid., 134.

5. David Blankenhorn, *Fatherless America* (New York: Harper Perennial, 1995), 226.

6. C. S. Lewis, *English Literature in the Sixteenth Century*, quoted in Stu Weber, *Along the Road to Manhood* (Sisters, OR: Multnomah, 1995), 74.

Chapter 3: Coming to Terms with the Past

1. Ken Canfield, *The Heart of a Father* (Chicago: Northfield Publishing, 1996), 28.

2. Monte Edwards, "Passing on the Wisdom of the Ages," *East County Gazette*, July 2003.

3. Dennis Rainey, "Keeping Covenants," in *A Life of Integrity: Twelve Outstanding Leaders Raise the Standard for Today's Christian Men*, ed. Howard Hendricks (Sisters, OR: Multnomah, 1997), 59–60.

4. Adapted from The National Center for Fathering, weekly email newsletter, August 20, 2004.

Chapter 4: Bonding with Your Boy

1. R. Kent Hughes, *Disciplines of a Godly Man* (Wheaton: Crossway Books, 1991), 47.

2. Gleaned from Robert Lewis, *A Journey into Authentic Manhood*, audiotapes of lecture "The Absent Father Wound," sessions 3–4, presented at Fellowship Bible Church, Little Rock, AR, 1997.

3. Preston Gillham, *Things Only Men Know: What Matters Most in the Life of a Man* (Eugene, OR: Harvest House, 1999), 82.

4. Gleaned from Lewis, *A Journey into Authentic Manhood*.

5. Ibid.

6. Ron and Matt Jenson, *Fathers and Sons: 10 Principles to Make Your Relationship Stronger* (Nashville: Broadman & Holman, 1998), 14.

7. Michael Gurian, *The Wonder of Boys: What Parents, Mentors and Educators Can Do to Shape Boys into Exceptional Men* (New York: Jeremy P. Tarcher, 1997), 122.

8. John C. Maxwell, *The 21 Most Powerful Minutes in a Leader's Day* (Nashville: Thomas Nelson, 2000), 43.

9. Michael Gurian, *A Fine Young Man: What Parents, Mentors and Educators Can Do to Shape Adolescent Boys into Exceptional Men* (New York: Jeremy P. Tarcher, 1999), 111.

10. Bryce M. Towsley, "Deer Camp Dreaming," *American Hunter*, Palm Coast, FL, November 2004, 47–50. Used by permission.

Chapter 5: Mistakes All Dads Make

1. This story was taken from Inspirational Christian Stories and Poems Archive, "Share Your Time," http://216.71.2.132/texts/topics/makeadifference/sharetime .shtml.

2. Joe Stowell, "Imitating the Father," in *A Life of Integrity*, ed. Howard Hendricks, 97.

3. Coach John Wooden, *Wooden: A Lifetime of Observations and Reflections On and Off the Court* (Chicago: Contemporary Books, 1997), 199.

4. Gary and Carrie Oliver, *Raising Sons and Loving It! Helping Your Boys Become Godly Men* (Grand Rapids: Zondervan, 2000), 139.

5. John Emerich Edward Dalberg, letter to Bishop Mandell Creighton. Louise Creighton, ed., *The Life and Letters of Mandell Creighton* (New York: Longmans, Green and Co., 1904).

6. Dag Hammerskjöld, *Markings* (New York: Ballantine Books, 1964), 88.

7. Stu Weber, *Spirit Warrior: Strategies for the Battles Christian Men and Women Face Every Day* (Sisters, OR: Multnomah, 2001), 127.

8. Hugh O'Neill, "Temper, Temper," *Parenting*, January 1995.

9. Hammerskjöld, *Markings*, 53.

10. Larry Crabb, *Inside Out* (Colorado Springs: NavPress, 1998), 98–99.

11. Os Hillman, "Humility in Relationships," Salt on the Net email newsletter, October 7, 2004.

12. Gillham, *Things Only Men Know*, 32.

Chapter 6: Making a Noble Man

1. Gillham, *Things Only Men Know*, 11.

2. Ibid., 89.

3. Blankenhorn, *Fatherless America*.

234

4. Al Covino, "Winners and Winners," *A 4th Course of Chicken Soup for the Soul* (Deerfield Beach, FL: HCI, 1997).

5. Adapted from Dennis and Barbara Rainey, *Moments Together for Couples* (Ventura, CA: Regal, 1995). Used with permission. Copyright 1995 by Dennis and Barbara Rainey. All rights reserved.

6. Adapted from Lisa Beamer, *Let's Roll: Ordinary People, Extraordinary Courage* (Wheaton: Tyndale, 2002).

7. "The Easiest Thing to Do Is Nothing," Inspirational Mail, 2001, http://inspirational mail.com/compassion/do.htm.

8. Ron and Matt Jenson, *Fathers and Sons*, 26.

9. Gillham, *Things Only Men Know*, 180.

10. C. S. Lewis, *The Abolition of Man* (New York: MacMillan, 1947), 35.

11. Gurian, *A Fine Young Man*, 239.

12. Ibid., 240.

13. Adapted from Gurian, *A Fine Young Man*, 239–40.

14. Gary Smalley, "Honoring Others," in *A Life of Integrity*, ed. Howard Hendricks, 58–59.

Chapter 7: Discipline

1. Gary and Carrie Oliver, *Raising Sons*, 137.

2. Joe White, "The Ultimate Challenge: A Life or Death Decision," Promise Keepers conference, Rose Garden, Portland, OR, August 2003.

Chapter 8: Loving Your Wife

1. Ken R. Canfield, *The 7 Secrets of Effective Fathers: Becoming the Father You Want to Be* (Wheaton: Tyndale, 1992), 126.

2. Rainey, "Keeping Covenants," 71–72.

3. Bill Bright, "Committed to Marriage," in *A Life of Integrity*, ed. Howard Hendricks, 79–80.

4. Rainey, "Keeping Covenants," 72.

5. Brent Curtis and John Eldredge, *The Sacred Romance: Drawing Closer to the Heart of God* (Nashville: Thomas Nelson, 1997), 74.

Chapter 9: Respect

1. James Dobson, *Bringing Up Boys* (Wheaton: Tyndale, 2001), 230.

Chapter 10: Sex

1. Christianity Today website, an article adapted from *Preparing Your Son for Every Man's Battle*. Copyright 2003 by Stephen Arterburn, Fred Stoeker, and Mike Yorkey. Used by permission of WaterBrook Press, Colorado Springs, CO. All rights reserved.

2. *Christianity Today* Leadership Survey, 2001, www.ctlibrary.com/9582.

3. Gurian, *A Fine Young Man*, 271.

4. John Eldredge, *Wild at Heart* (Nashville: Thomas Nelson, 2001), 43.

Chapter 11: Role Models and Mentors

1. Eldredge, *Wild at Heart*, 62.
2. Eveyln Bassoff, *Between Mothers and Sons: The Making of Vital and Loving Men* (New York: Penguin Books, 1994), 16.
3. Eldredge, *Wild at Heart*, 62.
4. Robert Bly, *Iron John* (New York: Vintage Press, 1990), 16.
5. Frank Pittmon, *Man Enough* (New York: G.P. Putnam's Sons, 1993), 16.
6. Canfield, *The 7 Secrets of Effective Fathers*, 4.
7. Gurian, *The Wonder of Boys*, 117.
8. Steve Farrar, *Point Man* (Sisters, OR: Multnomah Publishing, 1990), 41.
9. Gurian, *The Wonder of Boys*, 109.
10. Gurian, *A Fine Young Man*, 50.
11. Ibid., 72.
12. Gleaned from Robert Lewis, *A Journey into Authentic Manhood*, audiotapes of lectures "Promises at the Starting Line" and "Why Men Are So Confused Today," sessions 1 and 2, presented at Fellowship Bible Church, 1997.
13. Statistics obtained from a variety of sources, including: David Poponoe, American Family Decline, 1960–1990: "A Review and Appraisal Journal of Marriage and Family," August 1993, 55; U.S. Census Bureau, March 1998 Supplement to the Current Population; National Center for Health Statistics; and Cynthia Daniels, ed., *Lost Fathers: The Politics of Fatherlessness in America* (New York: St. Martin's Press, 1998).
14. Paul Zweig, *The Adventurer: The Fate of Adventure in the Western World* (Princeton, NJ: Princeton University Press, 1974), ch. 3.
15. Jim Brown, interview by Suzy Kolber, *ESPN Sunday Night Football*, ESPN, November 7, 2004.

Chapter 12: Leaving a Legacy

1. Eldredge, *Wild at Heart*, 122.
2. Christina Hoff Sommers, *The War against Boys* (New York: Simon & Schuster, 2000), 174.
3. Maxwell, *The 21 Most Powerful Minutes*, 89–90.
4. Stu Weber, *Locking Arms: God's Design for Masculine Friendships* (Sisters, OR: Multnomah, 1995), 41–42.
5. Damon Bradley, "On Not Letting Georgette Do It: The Case for Single-Sex Boys' Education," *The Vincent/Curtis Educational Register* (Boston: Vincent/Curtis, 1996), 5. See also Diane Hulse, *Brad and Cory: A Study of Middle School Boys* (Hunting Valley, OH: University School Press, 1997).
6. Gordon MacDonald, *When Men Think Private Thoughts* (Nashville: Thomas Nelson, 1996), 69–70.

Rick Johnson is a bestselling author of *That's My Teenage Son, That's My Girl, 10 Things Great Dads Do,* and *Better Dads, Stronger Sons,* as well as *Becoming Your Spouse's Better Half* and *Overcoming Toxic Parenting.* He is the founder of Better Dads and is a sought-after speaker at many large parenting and marriage conferences across the United States and Canada. Rick and his wife, Suzanne, live in Oregon. To find out more about Rick Johnson, visit www.betterdads.net.